One-parent families
a practical guide to coping

Diana Davenport, as a single parent, has brought up eight children. She has already published a book entitled *Adoption and the Coloured Child* and has wide experience as a journalist, at one time contributing regularly to the 'Femail' page in the *Daily Mail*. She has also written for other national newspapers and magazines including *Nursery World*, *Woman's Own* and *Woman's Realm* and has broadcast on radio and television.

Diana Davenport

One-parent families

a practical guide to coping

Pan Original
Pan Books London and Sydney

First published 1979 by Pan Books Ltd,
Cavaye Place, London SW10 9PG
© Diana Davenport 1979
ISBN 0 330 25865 6
Printed and bound in Great Britain by
Richard Clay (The Chaucer Press) Ltd, Bungay, Suffolk

Dedicated, with love,
to my raw material:

**John
Jackie
Jasmine
Sebastian
Helen
David
Andrew
and Kevin**

Contents

1 Introducing ourselves

Father + mother + children = the standard family; emotionally, practically and economically self-propelling. This may be the ideal unit in an ideal world. The children draw (mainly) from the mother – who is willingly drawn upon. She, in turn, replenishes this maternal cornucopia through her relationship with the father, who, in giving, also receives. It is an equilateral triangle.

Nine out of ten families in Britain present, at least potentially, this pattern of the regenerative Triangular Family. It is everyone's norm.

Mother alone (less often father alone) + children = the one-parent family; emotionally lopsided, practically limited, economically balancing on the high-wire. Such a situation has no place in an ideal world. The children draw from the mother, who is out at work/down at the Social Security/mending clothes/unblocking the drain. She, in turn, draws upon her own inner resources and creates an open-ended pattern of the least complexity.

One in every ten families in Britain is represented by this theoretically non-regenerative thread. We are the Linear Exception. Looked at in a cold light it could be pretty bad. Sometimes it is. Happily for us, more often it's not.

Like every other sort of human being the single parent falls into any of a hundred different character-slots. On the one hand a certain kind of mother is born to founder. No matter how much financial, material and personal help is meted out she's still going to fail. And by failing I mean she's going to grumble, feel sorry for herself, mismanage the housekeeping and forget to send her child to school with plimsolls on PE day. Even were she in a two-sided family she'd make a mess of it: running a one-sided family she has a ready-made excuse on which to hang the blame.

At the other end of the scale is the super-mother who earns, by luck, gift, skill or indefatigable hard work, an enormous salary, employs a nanny and has one or two children on purpose. She has the world taped anyway and is going to succeed whatever she is or does. This book is not for her.

Still, while perhaps not offering all that much lift, either, to the determinedly gloom-laden, I believe that the information between these covers may well help the thousands of 'ordinary' one-parent families which, like my own, veer querulously from high to low according to pressures both from within and from without. We usually get along, yet there may be new dodges to learn, new heights from which to fall headlong, once we are given the knowledge.

There are, in Britain, about 700,000 families with only one *functional* parent. The vast majority of these solo parents are women (which is why I may write as though we all were, and not merely because I write from my own female angle and experience): divorced, widowed, unmarried (having never been married), in that order. Also wives of men serving long prison sentences, and women with husbands away in hospital for months or years at a time, though perhaps not technically 'separated', will find themselves playing the part of double parent. Over a million-and-a-half children are involved.

Most single-parents have only a single child. Many have a couple. Some have three or four. A few, myself included, seem to keep on and on until people turn to stare in the street. (Indeed, Mrs S. of Hertfordshire has fourteen.) The basic tie is the same, however many, and we become adept at finding the best ways of coping both with our impoverished selves and with our progeny.

There are two distinct varieties of single-parent:

Firstly, those who decide of their own free will to create such a family from scratch, either by having a child – or children – independently; or by breaking from the matrimonial tie before that relationship itself becomes the breaker. Again, like my own octopus brood, it may consist of a mixture of children gathered up, so to speak, in passing; born within marriage or without it; adopted, or long-term fostered. We are essentially family for family's sake, and wanted, at that.

Secondly, those who are precipitated into sole-parenthood by death, desertion or divorce and who have the situation thrust upon them against their own choice.

These two groups present very different sides of a common position, especially at the beginnings of one-parenting. The former, in the main, tend to be more self-sufficient and to possess the ability to circumnavigate the loneliness bugbear (there has been, to a greater or lesser extent, a conscious decision to live without a resident male). This mother is able to make not only a silk purse out of a sow's ear (later I will explain how to cook a pig's ear, which is a good and cheap form of protein) but, far more to the point, create a decent skirt from the bathroom curtains, a go-cart from a redundant perambulator, or a day's outing from one of the excellent adventures that are still to be had for free. If she is often visibly buoyant it is because she extracts genuine pleasure from bringing up her children alone. She has had time gradually to build up her own method of one-parenting. Beneath that optimism there hides a sense almost of reprieve. As one mother puts it, 'All this (the responsibility of one-parenting) is the cost I pay for being "liberated" ... in a state of self-respect and therefore greater happiness than I have ever known before ...'

On the other hand, women suddenly left holding the baby (or older children) after bereavement are faced all at once with both grief and total responsibility. While others, abandoned with all maternal and household cares after the stealthy retreat of husband and father, are justifiably prone to panic and go under. How safe, after all, is the hitherto unshakable roof above her head? What about money, which, previously, automatically appeared in the housekeeping account? Will the neighbours understand? What will mother-in-law, father-in-law, granny, grandpa and Old Auntie say? ('Told you so!' most likely.) How to manage the imposed isolation, physical frustration, guilt pangs and solid fears? It can certainly look ghastly in first light.

Widows, swimming blindly through devastating sorrow simultaneously with the overwhelming number of practical and 'outside' decisions, begin one-parenting (without a doubt) under greater stress than anyone else. As with the deserted, they have had no time to anticipate life alone with the children, no period of acclimatization between one stage of life and the next. Of all the ways into the Linear Family position, that of widowhood is the most desperate.

The half-family has already supplied the bases for several deep and direct reports, and these reports are unwaveringly grey. We know, and accept, that statistics cannot in themselves lie, yet we should also realize that figures can be weighted A-wards or Z-wards. For instance compare '43 per cent of single parents depend to a greater degree upon Social Security payments', with '57 per cent of single parent families are partially or totally self-supporting', and see what I mean.

'One-parent families blighted from the start' states *The Times* Social Correspondent boldly, and the public is all too ready to pop us all, regardless, into another category labelled 'Minority Group'. I am exaggerating only in the mildest form when I suggest that many people see the one-parented child as *inevitably* inferior to his two-parented peers. He has baked beans on Wonderloaf for Sunday dinner. No presents. No holidays. His mother whines about the price of frozen haddock (having never been taught, poor ill-educated thing, to buy fresh coley) and the landlord (whose rent no doubt is overdue) complains – this time – about nappies drying along the window sill.

All right, some might see us as a brave lot; ever-struggling; dragging up the underprivileged as best we may in over-sized second-hand boots; yet membership of a one-parented family does not in itself lead unremittingly to a poor academic, emotional and material existence. My children get into the sixth form to work for A-levels all right; probably yours do too. There can't be any magic about the possession of both mother *and* father that guarantees 'a better chance'. 'Chance', here, is the important word.

There is, I'd be the first to admit, a certain bad breath of doom about rotten housing, persistently inadequate income, and boredom. Boredom, yes. Because boredom takes over under the guise of 'Can't be bothered' where hope is withdrawn. And single parents, individually, would spark up no hope at all if each made a meal of statistics instead of turning about to head into not only the self-help movement, but the help-one-another movement as well.

I would like to suggest that the majority of one-parent families can, do, or could work. Many of us *want* to bring up our children independently of both man and state. We *like* to earn the cash that keeps our households together. Our children *do* respond by earning their educational certificates, their Cub badges, their social invitations, just like 'ordinary' children with two parents. For parenthood is as much a mental as a material responsibility. It is our attitude, our management of matter and mind, that builds or destroys our future, and that of our children too.

It would be presumptuous to believe that my own family of eight could be an exception to the one-parent-downhill-spiral. Certainly we are not alone in our happiness. We want to be seen, though, as a participating, expanding unit, not as an exception to convention and not simply as a statistic on a government report either. However, to survive, to sustain this 'high', our lifestyle must always be positive and essentially non-acquisitive. We would do well to remember, when our thoughts wander perilously near the edge, that nobody *made* us take on this incredibly marvellous job of propping up our own families. Many of us *could* have stayed within the crumbled past of marriage 'for the sake of the children', *could* have had the baby aborted/adopted/fostered/put into residential care, could, indeed, have let the other half take custody, care and control. But we didn't. *Why?*

Further reading

The Finer Report, Volume I, HMSO (£3.15).
The Finer Report, Volume II, HMSO (£4.55).
Both available from Atlantic House, Holborn Viaduct,
London EC1 1BN, or from Sovereign House, St George's St,
Norwich, NOR 76A.

This mammoth Government-backed £206,332 report was completed in 1974. Only one quarter of its recommendations have, to date, been implemented. It is a work to peruse in the reference library rather than to buy, and rhetoric sometimes renders its matter indigestible.

Thus, try also:

Finer Report: Action and Inaction, Facts No. 1 (20p). From
The National Council for One Parent Families,
225 Kentish Town Rd, London NW5 2IX.

The Finer Report: Recommendations and Responses (65p).
For conference speeches by Barbara Castle *et al.* Available as above.

Growing up in a One Parent Family. A National Child Development Study, by Elsa Ferri (£3.85, by post £4.25). Obtainable from the National Children's Bureau, 8 Wakley St, London ECIV 7QE. This report compares the development and background conditions of 750 one-parent eleven-year-olds with 12,000 two-parent children born in one week of March 1958.

Coping Alone looks at the same group of children four years later. The author is here joined by fellow-researcher Hilary Robinson, sponsored by the National Foundation for Educational Research in England and Wales. The cost of the report is £1.15 (by post £1.80) and it may be obtained, again, from the National Children's Bureau.

2 Towards a one-parent philosophy

What, exactly, are we after? And how do we hope to achieve it? I mean on the personal, family level – not the national, campaigning, public side which seeks to alter official attitudes and legalities. All that is quite a different question.

Certainly we want to function as a 'normal' household. A normal alternative if you like. We want our children to feel on a par with their two-parented contemporaries. We want mental and financial independence (though the latter we're willing to take with a pinch of salt) and the freedom that goes with both these lovely states. We want, I suppose, happiness – like everybody else. Not necessarily a giddy, dizzy sort of euphoria, though a little of that isn't bad – but a steady run-of-the-mill balance which turns every day into a pleasant achievement. But we want, most of all, a good life for our children. A life looking outwards, unadorned by inessentials we can't afford to do or buy. What we are after, then, are the means to be marvellous parents without forgetting that we too are alive and well.

It sounds very ordinary, and that's the whole point. But how do we achieve such ordinary ambitions within our undoubtedly truncated family?

First, and this can hurt, we have to admit to ourselves that, however many thousands of us there are, however much we view our home life as an alternative norm, we are in fact depleted to the point of half. One head and two hands cannot do the same as two and four. Can we be in the house looking after the baby and out at work at the same time? Can we read to one child while bathing another? (Yes – just). Can we replace the split floorboard while simultaneously icing the cake? If we *are* going to be as efficient as our Triangular friends and neighbours we'll have to work at it twice as hard. We have opted to be mother *and* father, which is veering a little away from being mother-plus-mother. I mean that we will have to accept as a matter of course many roles which would, down the street, be the prerogative of father. Have you ever tried teaching your adolescent to shave?

Second, we have to stand back and take what people call a good look at ourselves. What can we *use* from time present or time past that will enable us either to make a living, create a better environment for the children or generally add to the length and breadth of daily self-sufficiency, both mental and/or material?

Consider the type of training or job experiences you had between school and now. See whether any of these, however rusty, can be utilized in conjunction with proper child care. See, better still, whether some specialization of yours can be practised from home, thus eliminating that mountainous question: 'Ought I to leave the children to go out to work?' Never mind if it doesn't bring in your full financial requirements (see chapter 5 for topping up a low income). The thing is to get going, to aim towards making some sort of an independent living, because this lifts the morale and pushes one forward into a little haze of confidence. I've known – still know – women who've made use of hobbies and sidelines in the absence of straight training. One makes beautiful toys at home, great floppy dolls which have gradually been accepted by more and more stores until, today, she brings in several hundred pounds a year through what began as making her daughter a doll out of odd bits and pieces. Several single-parents do indexing from home, hundreds more offer a typewriting service. I know at least two who take piano pupils, one who coaches reluctant O-level candidates, another who mends tennis rackets and porcelain at the kitchen table. All have gained by their efforts, and not only financially.

This self-examination is no time for doubt or modesty. Recognize what you've got, even if, initially, you think you've got nothing. For instance, I was fairly unpromising material at the beginning of one-parenting. Already I had plenty of children, but not, I thought, much that I could turn to practical in-the-home work. Then, as I comforted myself with the thought that I was, at least, an excellent mother, I realized that the solution stood before me, multiplied at that time by five. Years ago I'd trained as a children's nurse and had gone on to midwifery. I enjoyed young human beings and had patience and tolerance enough to stand up to the attendant roistering. The penny dropped. I had it made.

First I registered as a 'daily-minder', later I became a foster mother. Not much monetary feedback you might think, but in fact we manage to plough a little of the statutory allowance into general funds each month. Sometimes I take handicapped or 'difficult' children which gives a more generous allowance but is more taxing work.

Then, too, I was relatively literate. Writing fits into any old corner of the day and into the long one-parent evenings. I got a trickle of acceptances at first, and never exactly a flood, but enough money, together with cleaning and caretaking the church hall and a minute income which came – and still comes – magically from a Trust Fund, to render us independent of external aid.

And who, ten years ago, would have thought it?

Third, having put in order the more-or-less cerebral gifts and exploited all help-yourself possibilities, look *around* you instead of within. House, flat, yard, garden, roof even – how can you encourage these to work for the family too? Growing edible things is perhaps the most obvious first move, thus you cut down your food bill. Gardening isn't difficult so long as you do as the seed packet tells you. Keep the pigeons off too (I had a noisy baby once whom I parked on pigeon-duty near the lettuces), and if the children keep mice or hamsters bury their litter in the area where you plan to plant next. There are masses of seeds for health-maniacs on the market which can be grown indoors, so flat-dwellers are not entirely let off. Alfalfa is a sort of lightning cress. Beans will sprout in trays under the bed. Mushrooms, if you're prepared to be really attentive, will grow in a box under the kitchen sink (not if you own an indoor cat). The advantage of growing things is that the children join in. Mine sometimes sell their vegetables to our local green-grocer.

Self-justifying animals must surely come next. Given room and inclination, hens will produce blissful new eggs with warm shells and eye-shattering yolks. Have rabbits too, in fact anything you like, according to space. But be sure to keep pets-for-pets'-sake at a minimum, producers at a maximum. Always remember that the point of the game is to help yourself.

I know the majority of single-parents either aren't fortunate enough to have any ground, or they have jobs that leave little time for anything except essential child-loving and household chores. In that case, if there's a spare room, perhaps a self-contained lodger? Someone who cleans their own room, gets their own food, does their own laundry at the launderette (and might take yours too). There is money in renting rooms. But lodgers can also be boring/noisy/smelly/amorous; so limit yourself to temporary boarders, certainly at first; then you can count the days if they don't suit (see also p. 76). Depending on your geographical situation, you may well like to take paying guests for part of the year only. Holiday bed-and-breakfasts are lucrative if you're within reasonable distance of the sea, country-side, a cathedral city, race-course or an ancient monument. But, alas, even if you have been raised to trust people, you must learn to be wary of passing visitors. Always, always ask sweetly for rent in advance. You cannot afford to subsidize camera-strewn tourists.

If you're in a flat hardly big enough to grow mustard and cress on a face flannel, too cramped for any livestock bar the children's stick-insects, still keep your eye open for using what you *do* possess. When you go away, for instance, make the holiday a straight swap with another one-parent (see chapter 11), or mind a child for another working mother while your own children are at school.

Fourth, creating time enough to be two parents is important. If the stamina can possibly be mustered, adopt the Nine-Day-Working-Week. I've done this since the beginning of Linear activity and can now almost look back, like a cat, to more lives than one. The NDWW is created very simply, either by getting up two hours earlier than formerly or going to bed two hours later, and not just sometimes, but always. Those two extra hours are for *working*: I write, others may do tailoring, stitch lampshades, type theses or sweat over a correspondence course which will lead to a better job when the time comes. Fourteen extra working hours a week – two full working days if you pretend you do without lunch, and you're up and above other mortals with your week-plus-two. Make up your mind to expand *into* time. It's amazing how much more of it you discover once the odd corners are used up. Begin by counting as minus all the moments you sit about vacantly.

Fifth is Positivism with a capital P. It is a life-game, obviously not confined to the single-parent, but the single-parent, like others, will find incredible changes in achievement and motivation once play has begun. The point of the never-ending exercise is this: everything, but *everything*, we do or think or eat or say is either positive or negative; either progression or regression. I don't want to go into 'good' or 'bad', that's a matter of ethics. One man's good is another's bad, anyway. Positivism cannot help but move us forward a step; negativism can at best compel us to stay where we are, at second-best tip us backwards into the previous square. To be obvious: if I am two stone overweight and eat a Mars Bar, that is negative. If I spend those same few pennies on nappy pins which we need for the baby, that is positive. To waste hot water (electricity) or boil two small eggs in a large pan is negative. To Vim the bath with cold water and pop the eggs in the kettle which we need for washing-up water anyway is positive. You see? It's incredible how all our small chores gather up into forces which either bear us up or knock us down, and comforting to know that we have almost total day-to-day control over the basic trivia of our lives.

In relation to children the same 'decision' rule applies. So, I yell at the boy for knocking over his mug of milk, then stamp out to get a rag to mop it up. Possibly I throw the sodden cloth at the poor cat, who happens to be eating the sardines which I stupidly forgot to put back in the refrigerator – all so negative one ought to howl and gnash. I've shown myself up as non-understanding, nasty-tempered, forgetful and, to boot, physically ugly (a yelling mother is one of the most hideous sights on earth). On the other hand had I matter-of-factly asked the child to go to the kitchen and fetch a cloth, then shown him how to mop up the milk himself, I'd have been acting positively. In future he would have been able to cope with such accidents; the milk would get cleared up just the same and I'd have kept my cool. We all know, anyway, that children are careless at times and all houses with children beneath their tiles routinely suffer genuine accidents. Positivity, then, can help us check ourselves *before* the damage is done. For, when a child feels we don't love him (and he does feel this when we shout unfairly) we lose something very specially important both to him and to ourselves. Our great black lapses will undoubtedly descend from time to time. There are days when that marvellous positivity might never have been and failure is written in the dust on the bookshelves. We've only ourselves to blame if, then, the child rates us its infant equivalent of a short-tempered bitch.

Sixth, never lose sight of the fact that there are advantages in being a one-parent family. In our methods of child-rearing we hold *carte blanche*. Orderly or disorderly: it's our choice. Nobody's coming home at six o'clock to swear as he falls over the Lego in the hall. There is no threat such as 'Wait till I tell Daddy!' No wily child playing one parent against the other. If Mummy says no – or yes, come to that – that's it and there's no appeal. Emotionally, too, as the active parent we hold an advantage over the absent father (slightly different in the case of widowhood). Cyril Smith MP, one of three illegitimate children, maintains that the bond between a single parent and her child grows particularly strong. Certainly I think it can, but one must be tough enough to let go in time before too much emotional dependence becomes damaging.

Certain of the more tedious chores of marriage are spared us once we branch into the half-family. It's good not to be tied to his/her double-time. I was particularly happy to be relieved of pressing my husband's suits, ironing shirts, cooking a proper meal in the evening. Eating high tea with the children and being done with food and washing-up by half-past-six leaves time to be with those children, to read aloud to them, to play excruciatingly wild cricket, to make sure they wash their backs and ears, not to mention the less merry chores which have to be done very often after work hours.

While rightly blessing the advantages, however, never forget that they are mostly small ones and are to *our* advantage, not the children's. They, at least from a conventional point of view, still miss out, and we are the ones who must make it up to them. It should be within the powers of us all to make use of available help and resources – not least those from within ourselves – so that our families boast lively, expansive children, well-fed, reasonably clad and at peace with their sole parent. She can be a tranquil, presentable and interesting parent too;

tolerably self-sufficient and with time and enthusiasm enough to enjoy those children, for *if the parent is content and thriving after her own fashion, then her children cannot help but thrive in her wake.*

Remember, if despondency threatens, that the virtues of being part of a two-parent family are often counterbalanced by crippling marital tension and poverty of communication. It needn't be all that good on the other side of the fence, however it appears externally. In certain moods of happiness I can easily be pressured into *recommending* the half-family. No, obviously not for every woman; that would be crazy. But for women who are maternal, mentally independent and able to retain an air of emotional normality without the trappings of a full-time male, then one-parenting is tops.

See Appendix

British Tourist Authority

Gingerbread Holidays

National Childminding Association

National Foster Care Association

Open University

Singlehanded

3 Whose child? (and various other legal points)

Security of possession is of first importance. Nothing is more awful than the dread of having a child taken away; fear of his removal may swamp every other reasoned thought. So, *be certain of your rights over this child*. If those rights aren't clear, then take a solicitor's advice straight away. Sapping quarrels and emotional blackmail can drain every ounce of your emotional energy if the custody of a child remains undecided. Many children of parents living apart get used as instruments in vindictive tugs-o'-war. Read any newspaper and you'll see. If doubtful, the matter must be put straight, then you'll begin to relax and enjoy your offspring without hovering around him overprotectively. Remember that children of estranged parents *are* sometimes whipped away from the school gate, from a day out, from under your very nose by jealous, scheming or simply loving fathers, so don't listen to people who keep saying he'd-never-dare. He may. For everybody's peace of mind (which also means a reflected peace for the child) make the home ground legalized. This is the first necessary action.

To look at the various possibilities briefly then:

An illegitimate child (about 9 per cent of all births) belongs, in law and in custom, to his mother (even where his father's name appears on the birth certificate). Exceptions to this rule can only come about through the process of law. A natural father may, for instance, apply to the court for custody, care and control. However, provided that the mother wishes to keep the baby and is in a position to offer adequate care, then this paternal gesture would not seem to take the form of a real threat – certainly not in terms of care and control. The choice of the child's religious upbringing is also exclusively the mother's. The father may apply to the court if he feels strongly, but in fact he has no direct redress.

Illegitimate equals 'not born in lawful wedlock'. The mother may be a married woman (this is not a bland statement as there are variations on the married woman which I explain later on), or a spinster, widow, or divorcee. She may have been living with the baby's father in a regular household for twenty years, but that infant is still *hers*. If she leaves the man she may take the child along, without his sanction, as part of her own hand-baggage.

Illegitimate people are still discriminated against in law. No hereditary title may be passed down to such a son (not even if he's an adopted son either, which to me has always presented a curious anomaly, as adoption legitimizes a person). Though he is recognized as a bona fide claimant to inherit from the estates of both his natural parents (so long as some proof of paternity exists), he is not entitled to any claim to the estates of a grandparent or other close relative (on either side) unless specifically named in the Will, or unless reference is made to grandchildren collectively. Thus he has no claim if any relative (bar his parents) dies intestate.

A child born out of wedlock may be rendered legitimate if his mother later – never mind how much later – marries his father. A child is also legitimized when adopted either by strangers or by mother alone (rarely by father alone, though that isn't exactly an impossibility) or by one natural parent together with a new spouse.

If the mother is married at the time of her baby's birth – be it ever so tenuously – to any man either present or absent, but one who is not the biological father of the child, then that child, though technically illegitimate, may be registered as the husband's as long as he gives his consent. Sometimes the mother's husband knows he isn't the father though more often, it seems, he doesn't. Further, if that baby lives under the matrimonial roof for any length of time he may well be regarded in any future legal wrangles as 'an accepted child of the family'. On the break-up of such a family this extra-marital child can make for a lot of boggling litigation, the more so if he has erroneously been registered as legitimate.

Incidentally, any mother (married or unmarried) is at liberty to withhold the name of her illegitimate child's father when registering the birth.

May I perhaps put in here – if I'm not too late – that it's terribly important, if you feel you must enter the father's name, to be honest. It's easy to clam up and enter the baby as the son of your husband for the sake of future tranquillity, but if that hoped-for tranquillity doesn't ensue, then the drowning waters are deeper still. If in this mess – and I've been in this mess (among many others largely caused by funk and/or lack of forethought) – it would be sensible, at a moment when all sense disperses in electric panic, to order only a shortened certificate. This gives the child's name (not that of either parent) with date and place of birth. It's quite usual to ask for this abbreviated document: it's far cheaper for one thing, and is adequate for most (but not all) occasions at which a certificate has to be produced.

If, however, you have already made your own confusion it is possible to have a birth certificate amended – even years after the event, and sometimes there are pressing needs for this alteration to be made. Incidentally, my solicitor advised against confessing, albeit voluntarily, to perjury: he seemed afraid that I'd be arrested and led away from my starvelings. The local Registrar of Births and Deaths was a more useful counsellor: indeed, the story wasn't new to him at all. Post-partum women, apparently, make all sorts of muddles. This good and understanding man made sure, first, that I wouldn't be clapped in irons, then set me on the way to putting my house in order. It took many months to clarify: much detailed analysis was made of events encompassing that fraught period surrounding the child's birth. Kind anonymous men at The Corrections Department (the very existence of such a department halves the guilt) rendered this soul-baring tolerable.

My daughter's father died while she was a baby. I don't possess – never have possessed – any official or legal document irrefutably proving his recognition of her, and as far as the Office of Population, Censuses and Surveys is concerned love letters don't count, however fervent. So the best poor little X can expect is an official void where her father's name ought to be. My ex-husband has been obliged to sign an affidavit declaring that he is not her parent, though his name can never be deleted from the original certificate: a marginal note will alone explain the error. Not, in our case, perhaps the most ideal solution, but better than living with a storm cloud of perjury resting above the issue. Little X is fitted out with a certificate which is now at least half-truth in place of one which was undoubtedly half-lie.

Where a child's natural father is living, then the birth can, in the wake of affidavits from both men concerned, be re-registered as illegitimate. It seems crazily inside-out in a world where most are trying to re-register in the other direction, but sometimes there are compelling reasons.

To sum up, then, this far from unusual predicament: a married woman can register an extra-marital baby in one of three ways: (a) as her own only, leaving the father's column blank; (b) as the child of herself and the natural father (either surname) with the *written* consent of that father; (c) as a child of her marriage, a *legitimate* child, so long as her husband gives his *written* consent.

A legitimate child is, pretty obviously, one born to parents who are legally married to one another. The child is, indisputably their joint property as long as the marriage lasts: and one marriage in four, in Britain, ends in divorce. The responsibility for the child's care, control and financial keeping rests equally with father *and* mother. On separation, either straight or as a preamble to divorce, the question of custody and physical care must be met and agreed. It's no good making friendly plans between yourselves without the follow-up of legal arrangements: you may not always be that friendly, and his word against yours proves nothing. Still, wherever and with whomsoever the child eventually lands up, his legitimacy remains constant.

An adopted child, whether adopted by one parent or by two, is also officially legitimate.

Custody refers to the all-over say in a child's upbringing. It does not necessarily mean that the child is *living with* that person to whom custody has been entrusted. Indeed, it is common practice these days to grant *joint custody* to a father and mother who have once been married to one another, that is, so long as they both put in for it. Important steps like choice of school, religious upbringing, medical treatment of a more than minor nature, careers training and so on should be discussed together, but often are not. In theory permission for a minor to go abroad, to marry, to live away from the parent in whose care and control he has been placed, should be granted by both parents under such an order.

In practice it would seem that an absent parent, even though he may hold joint custody, very rarely 'interferes' with his child's upbringing. I know of several such fathers (and one mother) who never see, and seldom communicate, with their growing children. Partly it is the very absence itself that is responsible for this caring gap, partly the difficulty of communication through a 'third party': the erstwhile spouse.

Incredibly, a child of separated parents – even of divorced parents – can remain in a custody limbo indefinitely. I know a child of twelve who, though living with and wholly maintained by her mother, and rarely seen by her father, is legally in no-man's-land; and her parents parted when she was four years old. The dilemma facing the parents is this: *both* are so frightened of losing – and so unwilling to share – custody, that neither will take the first step towards proceedings. This particular situation arose after suggested arrangements were contested. The judge nevertheless granted the divorce, requesting that custody matters be subsequently settled 'in chambers' (a private hearing attended only by those parties immediately involved in the case). Neither party happened to be represented by a solicitor in court and there has been no pressure to bring the case forward. The mother now holds a sort of anarchical custody as the sole supporter of the child, though this position might not hold water if challenged on a formal level.

About one-quarter of all divorce cases involve ancillary proceedings in connection with care or custody of the children. This is without doubt the most painful area concerned with splitting up.

Interim custody may be granted to one parent pending the court decision, particularly in cases where there is fear for the child's safety – or the mother's. The first move is to consult a solicitor (or Citizens' Advice Bureau.) If you don't happen to be married to the father of your child, custody is – don't forget – automatically *yours*. Unless he chooses to fight.

In all custody cases the interests of the children gain precedence over any rights of the parents.

Care and control means the day-to-day feeding, washing, loving, reading-to, elastoplasting, cleaning-up-after, reprimanding and so on (indefinitely) of a child who *lives with you*. This order is utterly separate from that of custody. A child may be in the custody of one parent while being under the care and control of the other, or, indeed, of a separate party altogether. Ex-wives, so long as they want it and are not leading scandalously unsuitable lives, almost always get care and control. The maternal instinct, at least in the eyes of the judiciary, is a valid emotion.

To be fair, most fathers don't *want* care and control. They prefer to go out to work without facing the breakfast washing-up on their return, not to mention collecting the children from the nursery, giving them supper (after shopping for it on the way), bathing them, telling a bedtime story, cutting fingernails, inspecting ears, trapesing about with drinks of water, tackling the midnight washing, ironing, doing the ten o'clock potting and stripping the wet bed in the morning.

They are not idiots.

Access is a visiting card. It concerns the contact arrangements made, either through the courts or drawn up in black and white by solicitor's agreement, for the parent who doesn't have the responsibility for the child's daily welfare. This may be so many weeks or weekends a year, certain times within school holidays, days or even hours permitted away from home, or it may be 'free' access in which case the mother and father mutually agree on visits, outings and holidays as and when the time arrives. There need not necessarily be any pattern to the system.

Access, in tricky cases, may contain a clause stating that a visiting parent may not remain alone with his (or her) child. This is a pretty acid state of affairs and will only be put into practice if there's any real likelihood of harm. It may also be applied where there's a genuine risk of a parent absconding with his (or her) child.

Access may be altogether refused a father, say, who is, a habitual and noisy inebriate, a particularly violent man or a man who has already earned himself a history involving sexual offences against minors. If a parent refuses to abide by arrangements made by the court, or if he makes himself a perpetual nuisance on that score, then he's laying himself open to prosecution.

Unmarried as well as married fathers (or mothers) may seek reasonable access to their children. Grandparents, too, may seek to obtain access to their grandchildren.

Injunctions are generally served on a man (or woman) who is thought likely to harm, mentally or physically, either his partner or the children. Injunctions come in two sizes and the former is the more generally used.

A forbids a man to 'harass, molest or interfere with' his wife or children, but does not forbid him to live as part of the family. *B* forbids the man absolutely from entering the house (avoided whenever feasible as this renders him homeless, thus creating yet another social disaster).

Failure to abide by the dictates of an injunction amounts to *contempt of court*, and can still mean prison.

An Emergency Injunction can be obtained within twenty-four hours of, say, a physical attack. Indeed, as a final move a judge may order the police to arrest a man who unreasonably frightens or actually harms his wife, mistress or children.

Married or unmarried parents can equally protect themselves by such measures under the *Domestic Violence and Matrimonial Proceedings Act 1976*. If the position at home gets so bad that the mother actually flees with the children, then the court can, later, order the man out of the house so that his wife and children may safely return to live there. It's better, as I never seem to cease urging, to use a solicitor, but if you *must* advertise your independence then do-it-yourself injunction kits are, though you may not credit it, readily available. (See Appendix for purveyors of these.)

If *at any time* (before or after legislation) you become truly frightened for the safety of your child – or genuinely afraid that he may be taken from you – then you could seek to have him made a *Ward of Court*. This action is *immediately* effective, rendering the child 'safe' (in so far as any child can be 'safe') with the person currently caring for him. That person must, though, agree to abide by the court's eventual decision as to the child's care and custody. You can take action forthwith, via the Social Service Duty Officer, NSPCC, even request police intervention if desperate, though ideally do it through your solicitor.

It is expensive, but you're probably eligible for *Legal Aid* (see p.31).

If a child *is* removed from the entrusted parent then prompt action is essential. Unfortunately these abductions are most likely to happen either at weekends (after an outing or an overnight stop with the other parent) or in the early evening after school. Solicitors' offices (with rare exceptions) are then closed. Social Service departments and Probation Services are dormant, and the police may be unwilling to interfere in strictly civil (as opposed to criminal) matters. So what must you *do* if caught in this unthinkable maelstrom?

Through your local police obtain the telephone number of the Social Services Duty Officer, who should always (twenty-four hours a day) be available for immediate advice and action. Then, your solicitor, if he's half a caring man, should have divulged a number – even a series of numbers – through which urgent counsel may be obtained out of hours. If you don't have any emergency number, but think you may need one, ask now. There must be a Law Surgery or similar service within calling distance.

An emergency application may be made to a High Court judge at any time, including weekends or at night, for an order prohibiting the removal abroad of any child pending a court hearing.

It is possible to have ports and airports screened for certain passengers, and luckily lone men with small children are fairly conspicuous. The *Home Office* is in control of this, following emergency application. Once out of the country a child is no longer under the jurisdiction of the British courts. Northern Ireland and Scotland are out too.

Normally, a passport will be granted to a minor at the request of *either* parent, without proof of custody, unless a caveat has been accepted by the Passport Office. If you are worried, it would obviously be a comforting move to get your solicitor to set this proviso in motion.

Children under five are rarely issued with individual passports. The authorities would rather they were added to a parent's existing one. Any prior objection lodged would apply equally to this grafted type of application. If, however, your child already has a separate passport (though not in *your* possession) or is already included on a relative's passport, the most the Passport Office can do is keep a note on file for a period of up to twelve months. If the passport is returned to the office for any reason within that year then the objection will be acted upon.

Solicitors are expensive and (almost) indispensable: so you must find one who is efficient and trustworthy. Court procedure is confusing and, worse, intimidating. For the uninitiated it is like being flung into an alien culture where you neither fully comprehend the idiom nor the physical moves. Just read this quote: '... the High Court judge refused to listen to my side of the story after listening for an hour to my husband's. He told me I had to agree to joint custody, though I had brought up the children on my own for five years. When I complained to counsel he said the judge might lose his temper and I might be deprived of custody altogether if ...' A second example is a judge who remarked that it was nearly time for lunch so if there was anything else to discuss apropos the children then it must be 'fought out' (his words) at a different time and in a different place. No true picture of the position was drawn and again the wife, who was, as in the first case, the co-respondent, had no opportunity of putting her point of view. Joint custody was also granted to this father, who openly declined to contribute so much as one groat towards the maintenance of his four children and who rarely bothers to set eyes on them.

An able and concerned solicitor could have induced a very different outcome to both these cases.

Remember that this obligation to interpret legalities comes at a time when most parents are under severe emotional strain already. Remember, too, that the majority of orders resulting from legal action are irreversible. A mother can lose home, income, pension rights, goods, chattels *and children*: the future really does hang in the balance. So, unless you possess a mind of unfathomed depth, foresight, hindsight, second sight and plain cunning, please don't imagine you can deal with any but the most trivial of legalities on your own. Well, you *can*, but you'd be a fool to. And here I speak (again!) as an erstwhile fool.

Some solicitors are obviously better than others when it comes to matrimonial cases, so it's sensible to find out which ones are sympathetically inclined. Still, however much of an understanding father-figure he may seem, he's not a welfare worker. Every syllable he utters, letter he dictates, telephone call he dials, costs you plenty. (But see *Legal Aid* below.)

It is a fact that most lone parents contact the Citizens Advice Bureau or an organization such as Gingerbread rather than, initially, brave a solicitor's office. Solicitors, if you're unused to them, may represent formidable establishment figures capable of instigating unstoppable motion. Once the preliminaries have been made many parents feel they're bowled along regardless and largely unheeded – and it's being unheeded that sparks off despair or, nearly as damaging, panic. Litigation can stretch on over years: it ought not to, but it can. Contested custody proceedings alone have been known to drag on over five years. So, you see, it is terribly important that you select a solicitor who is right for your type of case. Recommendation is often made by friends, ex-clients of the firm most likely, or, if you literally don't know where or how to start looking, ask for advice at your local CAB. However, don't be afraid to complain if you lose faith in any given legal adviser: if you're dissatisfied with his treatment of the case there's nothing to prevent you changing to another. In fact around 16 per cent of all divorce cases do involve at least one change of solicitor.

Legal Aid is a seemingly bottomless pit of funds which may be drawn upon to cover legal expenses for anyone on a low income. Actually it doesn't have to be all that low, though the means-testing is thorough and vigorous. Apply for it direct through your solicitor, if he doesn't immediately divine the financial situation and suggest it himself.

Legal Aid is not available for meeting costs of an *undefended* divorce action. This type of sundering is seldom expensive anyway, and is quick and easy as well. In all other types of case – and here we're most concerned with those involving defended actions in relation to custody, care and control, and access – either the whole or a given fraction of the whole fees will be drawn from the Legal Aid fund, depending on your current income and assets.

Not all solicitors are ideological enough to admit legally aided clients, though the majority are. The CAB could tell you which firms in your area support the scheme: otherwise, look for this sign

which ought to be prominently displayed – in the window, for instance.

The Green Form Scheme is a variation on the same idea, though strictly to cover small problems. It may well be that your initial interviews dealing with basic advice could later be taken on by Legal Aid.

Any solicitor working the Legal Aid scheme will also undertake Green Form work. Applications should be made in the same way, although the interrogation is not nearly as lengthy.

The Citizens' Advice Bureau, commonly known as CAB, is just exactly what it says it is. Advice of all sorts, from that connected with consumer complaints to that involving the specifications of the law; personal and private, public and general: they know it all. 'They' are voluntary workers, highly trained after being chosen for their sympathetic natures and tough common sense. Almost every reference book, government pamphlet and legal statute is there on the shelves of the CAB office. Inquirers are seen one at a time in decent privacy, and everything you utter is in strict confidence. Use this marvellous free service.

Law Surgeries or *Legal Advice Centres* are free sit-ins, philanthropically run by groups of lawyers and open to all who care to use them. These lawyers will not provide detailed follow-ups nor will they 'take on' cases. They will advise on the wisest steps to take, where to take them or, indeed, whether it might not be best to tread backwards and forget the whole thing. The atmosphere of the Law Surgery is informal and unintimidating. Good for beginners.

A *Law Centre* gives not only initial advice, but also will handle a case from beginning to end, including representation at court (or tribunal) if required. These centres cater only for residents within their own catchment area. Check by telephone before turning up.

Further reading

Improving the Status of Children Born Outside Marriage, a booklet by J. Neville Turner, which compares recent legal reforms in England, West Germany and New Zealand. 65p from National Council for One Parent Families.

Guide to New Legal Aid is a *free* leaflet available from CAB, Law Centres or direct from the Law Society.

See Appendix

Apart-Aid

Action for Lesbian Parents

CAB

Corrections Department

Council for Voluntary Service

Cruse

Families Need Fathers

Free Representation Unit

Gingerbread

Home Office

Law Society

Legal Action Group

National Council for the Divorced and Separated

National Council for One Parent Families

National Society for the Prevention of Cruelty to Children

Network

Paddington Neighbourhood Law Centre (for injunction kit)

Passport Office

Rights of Women

Salvation Army

Charities Digest published annually, this book lists all charities in Britain and indicates where financial aid is available. You need *time* to get through this gazetteer. Go to the Public Library for an hour, or borrow from Social Services.

4 Housing

Don't keep moving about. Children need security of tenure; and children with only one parent need a stable background even more than others. Problems and worries, like bitterness, can't always be hidden and the comforting certainty of a home to rely upon means much. The two-parent child seems capable of floating round the world in a frail craft with no tangible adverse after effects. Our children have enough nonconformity without bizarre trips. We must not entertain the idea of walks across Europe or Australia and back by Land Rover and ketch. There are limits which, manless and with a child, we would be better to observe.

Personally I would urge all one-parents who *can* to get out of London. Get out of all large cities, unless you know for certain that you'd be changed for the worse or made miserable by the withdrawal of urban pressures and pleasures. Rents are lower in the country. Houses, supposing you're in a position to buy, are cheaper and the further north you go the cheaper they get.

People have time to be more caring when freed from the strictures of cramped living. In small communities everyone knows everyone else, and that helps too. Nevertheless, you'll probably be a novelty for some time. The brusque lady who runs the WRVS inquires about your husband's line of business just to make sure he doesn't exist. And having checked her point could well turn up next morning with a savoy cabbage or a pair of her grandson's good-as-new corduroys. People in the country are still charitable but mind you speak the truth, for, unlike town-dwellers, they are incurably inquisitive. If you're not really a widow your bluff won't fool anybody. Anyway, sooner or later the children will tell.

The country has worked for us. We moved into our present house without a stick of furniture, without money, without (for reasons never fully explained) eligibility for Social Security. We owned a bantam cock, a rabbit, a black cat and a selection of basic clothing. Not a bed, blanket, cooking pot or piece of crockery – for our flight had been precipitate and fraught. The house was dirty and bare. It lay, still lies, over three fields, with a cart-track approach which turns to glutinous Essex clay throughout the winter months.

The rent was very low and, when I had the luck to inherit a small amount of money, I traded the lot in for the freehold. A little over £5,000 bought us six bedrooms, a three-quarter-acre garden, independence, and a roof over all our heads for ever and ever.

In my early days of one-parenting there were half-a-dozen of us – five children and myself, and at first I left the two youngest with my friend Dot because of lack of bedding and so on. Dot, the dishevelled kindly mother of a girl who used to help in the house in my married moneyed days, lived in the smallest house in England: one dwarf room downstairs, one up. She'd bought this baby house many years before for £200 and had reared her own daughter single-handed in it. Dot was full of sympathy. She'd been through it herself.

Never was anything in that little house relegated to the plane of rubbish, so at my first murmured begging Dot was able to heave an ancient flock mattress from the bursting shack in her back yard. She added a flame-coloured quilt, a couple of army blankets, a teapot (indispensable), a poker, a hatchet ('No need to buy coal, dear, go round the hedges for firing'), a pair of handleless cups and an aluminium fish-slice. From this nucleus we built up our home. *Never be ashamed to accept second-hands.*

The older children and I scrubbed out our new house. We swabbed it down like a ship's deck, scouring with stiff yard brooms borrowed from our farmer-landlord. The combination of warm water and warm weather woke the hibernating fleas: one saw them everywhere, leaping frenziedly, mad for humans' blood. For weeks we scratched, trying one proprietary pest powder after another, too delicate-minded to tell anyone, ashamed of our parasites.

I've since discovered that the Environmental Health Department (local council) is empowered to deal with fleas and their relatives as well as rats, mice, cockroaches and ants. So if you move, as we did, into an infested house – or if you acquire fellow-travellers by the way – you can, for free, get purified.

New friends soon produced old beds. The landlord arrived

with two tables on his trailer. Dot's neighbour came with another table and some chairs. Two strangers from the village walked over one evening with curtains and rods. A sofa with the ghost of springs, four dining chairs, several part-worn carpets, a tiny chest-of-drawers and an inaccurate bathroom scale swelled our inventory of worldly goods. By Christmas, when the local doctor arrived at the door with toys, I gave in to tears of gratitude.

Everyone seems to have stuff they are anxious to get rid of. Dustmen are at liberty to refuse any object too large for a bin, so we outcasts are sometimes heaven-sent opportunities. Even now, years after our leanest times, I am sometimes stopped in the village street and asked if I'd like a mattress, good as new with only one little stain; and I apologize, explaining that I have, unbelievably, enough of everything for the moment.

So don't be afraid. If you have the luck, as I did, to get into a real house, and you haven't a bean in your pocket or a pile of furniture in store, put your fortune in the lap of the great human race. Move in, children, animals and all. They won't mind camping; but try to do it in the warm weather. And don't be afraid to go out to make friends when they come, as they will come, three-quarters of the way to meet you. Endeavour, though, not to let the informal camping run on into a permanent fact of life. Meals balanced on a thumb are all very well but I know a girl who found to her discomfort, when she grew up and met the world, that she didn't know *how* to sit down to eat with civilized folk. She and her mother had been constantly in flight, cases packed, taking breakfast off the window sill.

Aim for living in a house, especially if you have more than one child. It gives you room for privacy, for spreading out sewing or wet washing or complicated cookery. Also it is more than likely to have a garden, or a yard; somewhere to potter, to let off steam; to keep a pet or a bicycle; to make a vegetable patch or heap the coke.

In times of hardship (and these will recur as do the tides) your house can also earn an income. Take in French students for the summer, Japanese businessmen for conferences, bed-and-breakfasting tourists. Or, if you don't like strangers sleeping in your sheets, daily-minding (like a mini nursery) or fostering, at the discretion of your local Social Services Department. So, if there's *any* chance of a house, take it.

*

Even if you have to share.

Sharing a house can be fun or hell. It's often the only way for a single parent to be able to afford one. What a pity that the great majority of single parents are mothers: six mothers to every father at a fair estimate. House-sharing could otherwise become part of a wider exchange, but it sometimes does. There's at least one agency which undertakes the finding of partners for would-be home-sharers. Good matching is made: personality, background, ages of children (pages of questionnaire), and the agency – itself founded by a one-parent – has a high success rate. It's called *Single-handed*, gives an excellent individual service, but makes a stiffish charge. Address, as with the rest, is in the Appendix.

A sharer can also be sought through advertising, or through associations like *Gingerbread* or the *National Council for One Parent Families*. But don't just barge into a share without getting to know a good deal about one another. Better to move in on your own (supposing you're the one with the house) and be poorer for a bit than rush into an ill-lasting partnership you'll regret before the second month's rent's due. The same temperament, same income, same tastes and an easy tolerance of one another's children are good ground upon which to build.

And be prepared, if you publicly advertise, to receive replies from a wide range of unsuitables in addition to a thin pile of possibles. Offers of instant marriage from incurable recidivists and alarmingly sane letters from unbalanced con-persons are quite usual. I once received a grubby fiver as a sort of deposit from a man who promised, in ill-spelled phrases, to send my many children to the best public schools and to give me double glazing. One really cannot, at a blank point in one's own life, stretch to the rehabilitation of others as yet unknown. Unadventurous as it may seem, it is better to stick to another one-parent and forego the treats.

Before you join forces with whoever seems the most likely choice, it's best to decide how you're going to split outgoings. It's no good magnanimously agreeing to an even distribution of expenses before you know what the other person's idea of normal expense is. I mean, it's hopeless to discover at the end of the first week that the other children will eat only muesli at heaven-knows-what a helping while yours are used to economical porridge. Even small unfairnesses like this, repeated day after day, can turn the best of us sour and unspeakable. It is perhaps most important of all to share basic ideas on the upbringing of children. It's sensible to give the thing a trial run on almost a holiday basis for the first month, then discuss the long-life possibilities of the enterprise. The parent who owns the house must arrange, through a solicitor, for some sort of written agreement to be drawn up. This is her/his safeguard against trouble. She/he might also like to read some of the pamphlets noted at the end of this chapter.

I know two women, with seven children between them, who shared a furnished farmhouse. It sounded magical on estate agent's paper, but was remote and cold with no paid work in miles. Both were academics, yet the only employment they could find was Home Helping for the council. One worked in the mornings, cleaning up after a nice old lady who provided mouldy cakes at elevenses and kept her savings in a Mason's Stores carrier under the mattress, the other worked during the afternoon for a farmer's wife with multiple problems. The baby-minding and chores at home were taken turn and turn about, but there never seemed to be time for anything apart from making ends meet. After twelve months what had started as a challenge in breathtaking scenery became an almost impossible drag of no money/no work/no time/and – worst of all – no stimulus.

'We never had enough time to ourselves,' says one, 'and although there weren't actually any quarrels we both knew we'd be better off with walls of our own. All the same, it was life-saving to have another adult there during the first months out of marriage, when litigation was brewing up fears – when the children were still bemused – and when, against reason, one nervously expected to be pursued by the man from whom one had fled. Now, miles apart, we have an unwritten agreement that, in emotional or other emergency, we'll help one another with shelter or funds as available. We're better friends now than when we were sharing that house.'

Sharing with another woman, anyway, is much more difficult than sharing with a man. A man need not become a lover, need not feature under the old Cohabitation Rule. One forty-year-old mother of four shares a large house with a distant male cousin who is 'just a very good sharing person . . .', this after a fraught period with another single mother during which the relationship steadily deteriorated, almost of its own volition. 'With women,' she sums up, 'you must be prepared to give a lot more.'

For combining on a long-term basis I imagine you would have to come to an arrangement whereby each had some separate family places. There must be a certain amount of escape line: room in which to be solitary, to give special loving time to one's own children, to give way to clouded depression.

It's interesting to note that the seven children of the farm-house mothers obviously found sharing easier than did the two adults. While managing to keep separate identities they threw themselves into the extended family with verve. It does seem true that children growing up in a community atmosphere learn to regard every other child as sibling, every adult as parent. Magnificent loving. But I am a jealous parent.

I used to imagine *caravans* as rock-bottom until I came to know one. In fact they can provide quite an adequate home for an independently minded single parent with a limited number of children. A second-hand caravan may be picked up from a holiday park very cheaply: you can even get one through a dealer (thus eliminating the problem of towing the thing away from its former site) for under a hundred pounds. So a caravan, provided you have a plot on which to rest it, is (following a term of judicious saving) within the grasp of the most impecunious among us.

If you don't know of a grassy verge, advertise. Choose a part of the country you're happy about and put a notice in the local paper. Offer yourself as a home help, handy-person, secretary, child-minder, girl groom, gardener, any service which fits your particular talent, and set this offer against free-parking-plus-moderate-wage. Prefix your advertisement with a 'sensible' adjective such as mature, quiet, responsible, dependable, and conduct any resulting interviews with care. People who have land enough to offer you caravan space can become marvellous friends/patrons. I have reports of several Linear Families who, in the nicest possible way, live comfortably off the massive crumbs from rich tables set, all right, against a measure of decent work.

One mother took on the job of looking after a deserted old man in exchange for parking her caravan in his wilderness. She toiled away for two years, fighting cobwebs, coaxing him to change his underwear, tracking down his ever-lost false teeth, cooking endless bread-and-milk and sago puddings. He left her both his debts and his crumbling home, the one burden was cleared, eventually, by running the other as a holiday guest house.

Rates, incidentally, are payable on a residential caravan, whereabouts immaterial (unless, gypsylike, you move ever on). These would be fairly minimal. Contact your local valuation office for assessment.

The living-in job is another beginning. Whether you start off as a one-parent with a new baby, or from a failed marriage with an older child, or as a widow with responsibilities, a period of 'living-in' is a period of time given over to adjustment. No worries about where the next meal's coming from or how the rent can be met, the boiler mended or the hall redecorated. The emotional upheaval of going-it-alone with the added tie of a child can be exhausting, and an unintellectual job in the line of housekeeping or mother's-helper might just be the life-saver you need.

For the more easily smothered person a similar job in a hotel, residential Home or the like might well work out. But, apart from exceptional instances, these live-in posts should be viewed as a stop-gap, a pool in which to tread water quietly before branching out independently as your own semi-family.

One exception to the stop-gap rule is, of course, a job in a boarding school – teaching if you've the qualifications, or being a matron, housemistress, or domestic supervisor. This is a comfortable answer to a mother left with an older child. The child is likely to receive free or greatly reduced board and tuition, while the mother receives a salary. Educational trusts or certain employment agencies could help with finding such work which is not hard to secure so long as you fit into the right category. Some magazines are marvellous for what are called 'institutional' jobs. *The Lady*, for instance.

Women with more than a single child stand little chance of finding residential employment. However, for those multi-mothers who insist, something like the personal column of the *Statesman* might just strike gold. Or, for a clergyman (more likely to have a housekeeper than any other professional) try the *Church Times*.

If you land a job with a shy bachelor or a lonely widower (particularly a widower with children) he might even marry you and take on the child as his own before the first year's through. It happens again and again, and is, indeed, one of the easiest-planned escape routes for an unwilling one-parent. Results are almost always tranquilly happy.

Having the courage to seek him out is probably the hardest part. Your motive is pretty obvious.

The bed-sitter is a gruesome start for a single mother. It is, obviously, preferable to having no roof at all, but life in one room (in particular if you don't go out to work) can be so oppressive that you may be driven into the more gruesome regions of your mind. Neither can you escape from the child, even at night. Nor he from you. Your radio, light, rustling book, clattering washing-up (in the hand-basin where you probably wash him and his nappies too), all these and more are set to disturb him. His crying may worry other people besides yourself and this, too, leads to grumbles. Babies also smell nasty quite a lot of the time. They are not good room-mates.

Bed-sitters, remember, can be almost as expensive as a small flat, so a half-or-less share of a larger place would be a far better thing to go for. Obviously you may have to take a bed-sitter as a desperate measure, but get on to something bigger, or at least more divided, as quickly as you can.

A flat isn't terribly easy to find in a hurry. Unless you're rich – in which case almost everything is terribly easy. Two-thirds of all flats are in the private sector. So gird yourself well before going out to search. Many landlords who might in private life be reasonable, charming men, will not entertain the idea of children dwelling in their halls. They are also frightened, since the *Tenancy Act 1967*, that once in you will never get out. They may be right. So be diplomatic in your hunting: look the part of the good tenant: appear neither impoverished nor feeble. Look the man in the eye, and smile. Don't give him a chance to say no. Once in, sit tight.

For a *furnished flat* you will probably be asked to put down a deposit against breakages, unpaid gas/electricity or avoidable damage to the property. This may be equated with, say, a month's rent. The landlord is quite at liberty to ask for this (he'd be a fool not to), but be sure that you get his written undertaking to refund it – or part of it, as applicable – when you move out. (If you haven't got a big enough lump sum, ask the local Department of Health and Social Security – even if you are not drawing Supplementary Benefit.)

If the flat is *unfurnished* you may be asked to pay something called 'fixtures and fittings' (curtains, etc) and you will also be responsible for paying rates. On the other hand you sometimes get free hot water and heating, more particularly if it's what's called a 'mansion flat'. It is illegal for a landlord to ask for a deposit against the letting of an unfurnished flat, though rent will often be required quarterly in advance.

Furnished or unfurnished, you cannot be forced to move out nor need you even go willingly without at least one month's notice. If the landlord does put on the pressure, look first at yourself and decide whether he has a reasonable complaint. A nappy pail on the landing, toys on the stairs, children shrieking until midnight? If you want to stay, and at a pinch acknowledge you may have stretched the limits a fraction, it's worth eating humble pie, promising instant reform if he will let you stay on. If however, he just seems to be bloody-minded about it, and you really haven't anywhere else in the country you can decently move to, then the law's behind you if you want to stay put. The landlord will have to apply for a County court order to evict you. Meanwhile go to a solicitor for advice. All this gives you plenty of time to look around for somewhere else if the worst happens. You can bet on a two-month lag between notice to quit and the court decision.

Should the landlord try a freelance eviction you're entitled to call the police because that landlord is, in effect, guilty of a criminal offence.

If he causes harassment indirectly, such as suspending supplies of electricity or water, or by creating noise through an adjoining wall, or endlessly sending workmen in to do needless repairs, then he can be taken to court.

If you can't find anywhere to lay your head, the council is obliged to re-house you. For you will then rate as a bona fide homeless family.

It's good to remember that the Housing Department can help with *rent and/or rate rebates*. You fill in a means test and they assess the amount for which you are liable. The income level below which you benefit seems, to my cheese-paring mind, remarkably high.

The Housing Department can also deal with 'unfair rents' in privately rented cases. This may mean attending a Rent Tribunal, but it's worth gunning for a reduction if you honestly feel that the landlord's pocketing excesses. But, before you make so much as a move in that direction, have a good think about the man's overheads, in terms of maintenance and dilapidations. What, in fact, is he having to pay out in order that you can keep that roof over your head? It's easy to see the rent you pay as pure profit: it's not.

However, if you do put in for a reduction you must accept that this is tantamount to declaring open war. You may well be in the right and you may well win a reduction, but the atmosphere will be charged for evermore. This is neither here nor there if you don't actually live in the same building as the landlord. But if you have to face him day after day as you pass him on the stairs the situation could wear you to bone. Some families will move on from grabbing landlords rather than fight this tetchiness. There's nothing to stop you putting in a word if you feel strongly about protecting the next tenant.

If you're drawing Supplementary Benefit, any rent, private or council, will be covered; but an allowance for rates is included in the weekly packet, so mind you save it up, for you're not then eligible for rebate. People who persistently make a mess of their finances – to whom budgeting is as foreign as a distant shore – can get their rent paid direct if they're in council housing.

Please note that no landlord (or anyone else) may ask for your Child Benefit order book to set against rent arrears or any other debt. This used to be fairly common practice, especially, for reasons unfathomed, in the north of England.

Council flats are available for single people with children, but qualifications vary with locality. Some boroughs still employ the 'points' system, which weighs against the one-parent family because an adult scores more than a child. Other areas stick to the residential qualification, with generally two years' rating as the minimum below which your name may not be added to the waiting list.

London boroughs are way ahead. Anyone may ask to be

added to the list in any given area on the very day they set foot in the capital. This doesn't carry any guarantee that a flat will be offered straight away, nor even quite a long step ahead; but it's a beginning.

Avoid the heady incarceration resulting from life in a high-rise flat. Battery living breeds neuroses. Accept such an un-natural habitat only in the absence of any alternative choice. And view it as an interim housing plan.

Some councils used to adopt a self-righteous attitude towards unmarried mothers. This, so far as I can gather, is quite out of date. No longer, as in the past, is a woman obliged to undertake to 'behave herself' as a condition of occupying council property. 'We are not a court of morals,' said one local manager. 'Each applicant is assessed according to need.' Nice to know.

Some places have dauntingly long lists – years of waiting perhaps – because so little new building is being done. Vacancies usually depend upon old tenants dying or families moving from the locality: relatively few council flats are first-time-round. Much more hopeful is the application made for a house or flat in a rural area or a New Town (Peterborough and Haverhill, at the time of writing, are well dotted with vacant council property). Waiting time can be a mere six or eight weeks in some cases. But whatever you want, waste no time: go to the Housing Department to see how the list looks, and if any hope's extended, put your name down.

There is no security of tenure with council property (they *may* evict you for such as persistent non-payment of rent or persistent nuisance-making to the neighbours) but it's fairly fool-proof so long as you fit in with the crowd. In any case they have to give you four weeks' notice, and they are also bound to offer you alternative accommodation, though this will probably be sub-standard housing.

If you get a nasty man at the Housing Department remind him that, under the *Housing Act 1957*, councils are obliged to give 'reasonable priority' to families who are 'occupying insanitary or overcrowded houses, having large families or existing under unsatisfactory housing conditions', which might just about be interpreted to suit your case.

Lone parents can be kept waiting in the queue for ages. Often it helps to take a friend along to the Housing Manager's office, for company can give one the courage to speak up instead of being meekly squashed. If things are desperate then you must make him understand that your case is urgent. I have known a single parent crack the horny exterior of a local housing official by way of correspondence with her MP. Within days a three-room flat above a grocery shop had magically become available where none, apparently, was available before. So don't accept the negative: go on and on trying and, sooner or later, you will succeed.

Twilight, half-way or plain sub-standard dwellings are generally Grade Z with a bit of life in them, or houses standing in the way of future development. Some boroughs will put families who don't yet qualify for the housing list – or those who, although on the list, can't be found a proper place – in these condemned buildings, and sometimes it is bearable. (More bearable, anyway, than a hostel for the homeless, where your soul may not be considered your own.) In the absence of any other immediate possibility it's worth bearing up to the damp, the third-rate plumbing and the bulldozers crawling ever nearer in order to fix upon the certainty of permanent housing as a sequel.

Hostels and bolt holes for the desperate exist in greater numbers than one is often led to believe. Many are run by charitable or religious institutions and there may be Rules. Some are private families who make a point of keeping a bed or two spare. Others are emotionally chilling; sometimes ex-workhouse property. A royal few are home-from-home in the most coveted sense. Single fathers with their children are welcomed in some but not all; schoolgirls with babies in tow are offered continuing education in others. Most of the council/charity/religious-run hostels are open only through the channels of individual Social Service Departments: I mean, parents themselves may not apply direct which cuts out the element of instant succour. Every Social Service Department should possess a list of hostels and refuges both in their area and beyond. If a homeless single parent meets with a blank she should urge her social worker to buy a comprehensive directory of short-stay accommodation from the National Council for One Parent Families. Temporary bed-and-breakfast accommodation is sometimes arranged by local councils for homeless families.

Special accommodation for one-parents, longer term, is nothing like as accessible (though neither is it, as some would have us believe, non-existent) as in, say, the Scandinavian countries, where single mothers are positively coddled. My Danish friend was provided with a lovely flat after the birth of her son sixteen years ago. It had a washing room; pram park, and a crèche in the basement. She's always been given the opportunity to hold down her full-time job, and thus retain the dignity of financially keeping herself and the child. Personal allowances have been geared to meet her special responsibilities, and even now, with the boy a great hulking Dane on the brink of taking on the world, there's a maximum percentage of earnings above which her rent may not rise.

The single mother in this country is lucky indeed if she finds a special flat or even a bed-sitter with what are called 'shared facilities' (kitchen, bathroom, laundry room, and some-times – very rarely – day-care for her child). For every thousand one-parents there is about one such special earmarked unit of accommodation. So, you see, chances are minimal. On the other hand, somebody has to have them, so it's always worth making a nuisance of yourself at the Social Services. London has around one hundred units. The north of England seems to have more than average. Other areas have some places, but duration of permitted stay varies from borough to borough. Some move in tenants on an indefinite basis, others stipulate 'no children of school age' or 'none under two' which obviously cuts through a good many parents' plans. Stays of six months, twelve months, two years, are frequently quoted. Again these special places are nearly always allocated through a social worker. So get working on her/him. Many organizations are willing to consider one-parent tenants from areas other than that in which their houses or flats stand.

Housing Associations are often biased in favour of one-parent families. Some cater exclusively for us. Generally they recog-nize that families with two or more children are hardest hit, so special efforts are made to include larger – sometimes split – properties.

One of the most depressing voids is that hole in time which

floats between joining the council list and actually being offered a house or flat. Six months, twelve, eighteen, more. Your guess is as good as anyone else's. This is where a Housing Association can help by providing fill-in accommodation pending the real and permanent thing. Indeed many associations make it a condition that tenants' names *must* be placed on the council list, thus ensuring a fall-off so that as many families as possible may be helped over the years. A Housing Association can be approached straight, without recommendation by a welfare authority, and this gives future tenants at least a sense of free choice and independence. A marvellous 'extra' included along with some accommodation is a service of help or sitting-in when a child is ill, or meeting and caring for children between 3.30 and 6 p.m. – that gap between end-of-school and mother coming home from work. There is, certainly, a hint of hidden social work afoot behind many housing schemes, and this isn't a bad thing so long as it promotes self-help and ultimate independence. Housing associations are self-financing but non-profitmaking, therefore rents are low. They generally work on the basis of buying and converting old properties, often dividing them into several flats or bed-sitters. The idea is fairly widespread up and down the country and nobody is barred from applying, although some very difficult, problem-ridden, anti-social families may be considered too tough to handle for the sake of the other tenants' peace. Advice on housing and finance will always be given free.

Special hostels for battered wives are less rare than they used to be. These houses are in the nature of lightning escape routes rather than permanent solutions; the alternative to going back to face the smasher for the sake of sheltering yourself and the children under his roof. Erin Pizzey is the forceful lady behind the London crush houses. Birmingham already has two. Others are slowly and sometimes a bit reluctantly coming along, some under the auspices of local authorities. Anyway, the need has been recognized. And you will never be turned away, even if there is no room at all.

It's interesting to learn that at least half of the sheltering wives decide, voluntarily I suppose, to pick themselves up and go home again.

If you're miles and miles from any known refuge when absolute homelessness strikes, ask the local police to contact Social Services. There's a Duty Officer on call over weekends and out-of-office-hours, and he can direct emergency action. The hardest thing that can happen – and it is bad – is that the council may take your child 'into care' temporarily so that he, at least, may be properly sheltered and looked after. No council should split families on the sole account of homelessness, though occasionally this does still happen in order to provide the only available shelter. Rest happy that you will have parted from the child under what's referred to as 'Section One', which means you have the right to request his return when you again have a home to offer him. There's no chance of him being kept from you, or being funnelled off into the long-term fostering band, or being made over to some old dear who's grown attached to him.

With such tiny comfort you may feel able to depart to some bed-and-breakfast establishment ('No Children' of course) to lay down your own weary bones. A gloomy, awful day if it comes to that. But some parents do – not only the 'inadequate' ones – and at least it's preferable to the great and lonely outdoors. With warmth and rest you can take a new look at tomorrow, while The Welfare, which is largely composed of fallible women much like yourself, will gladly help you look.

The mother who is bundled without ceremony into one-parenting, the woman who is left with baby, bills and mortgage, can now be helped to *stay in the matrimonial home*. Or to return to it. Luckily the law looks kindly, since the *Matrimonial Homes Act 1967*, upon the parent who is in sole charge of children and mortgage. Whether the pile was bought jointly or not, the chances of being able to take over are good. Even if you have been thrown out by your erstwhile loved one, you can still hope to return. If you haven't contributed a penny towards the purchase price of the years-long mortgage repayments, take heart just the same; your efforts to keep the place going, time and application spent in the boring old chores of cleaning windows, painting the banisters, stirring the soup, all count in as time lost from earning a wage outside the home. You are entitled to consideration as co-owner. Even if you are the one to 'break the marriage' by leaving home to squat with friends while he enjoys the freedom of twelve rooms, there's still a chance you'll be able to get back, if that's what you really want. Practical questions like keeping up the mortgage and possibly paying back your husband the other half of the money may produce insuperable blocks, nevertheless, it's worth finding out. What's best for you and, more particularly, what's best for the children, is given decent priority. Fighting this sort of case can be fraught, so get on to a solicitor to register your rights straight away or precious time will be wasted.

If your solicitor doesn't come up with the suggestion himself, inform him that building societies are often willing to accept, for the time being, 'interest only' payments, and that these can actually be met by a DHSS allowance until financial equilibrium is re-established.

Rented accommodation, with the exception of council property, can be transferred wholly to the name of the parent left with the children.

Cheering news for *unmarried* mothers is that even if your lover (or ex-lover) owns tenancy or freehold there is nothing to stop you putting in for residential possession of the property for yourself and the children in cases of intolerable behaviour – notably 'battering'. He can, literally, be obliged to leave his own house for you. You would obviously need legal advice on this.

Supposing, now, that you want to buy another house on a mortgage rather than prop up the old memory-riddled one, contrary to popular myth there is no bar to a single person, with or without children, taking on a new mortgage. True, some building societies are more sympathetic than others, and no two have identical 'house rules'. If you've been saving through any particular society in the past, then they are likely to give you preferential treatment, though naturally there's no guarantee of a loan. Everything hinges upon the combination of your age, earning capacity, stability of job/income and the level of your commitments, family and otherwise. The generally accepted yardstick is an advance of two-and-a-half times your basic annual income.

The best advice I can give is to shop around the various building societies before you commit yourself to any given one. See what they have to offer, how civilly they regard you and how spontaneously available is detailed advice. If you're in reasonably paid work and have savings of several hundred (even unsupported mothers may have savings, for thrift grows like moss upon us) then a mortgage could easily prove your best housing bet.

There's no central organization geared exclusively to giving advice on mortgages, though most general help centres – CAB, SHAC, Housing Aid, etc – use experts in the field.

Simply staying at home with your own parents is quite a reasonable thing to do so long as you get along well and they are wholeheartedly behind the idea. Remember, it's probably a long time since they had a baby in the house. About a quarter of all one-parent families do just this, mainly unmarried women who never have had a home of their own, and fathers left with the children. Difficulties can and do crop up. Granny gets domineering about methods of child care. Grandpa brings a lollipop home every evening and ruins the little milk teeth. These problems can be solved with tact; so when depressed, cheer yourself by weighing up the debits against the credits of living under the family roof – for both of you. If you're a fairly pliant sort of person it may well be easier to submit to the baby being dandled on auntie's lap when in fact you would have him asleep in his cot. For, once the grumbles have been given expression they multiply, and no disagreements are more hurting than those among the family.

It's very useful to know that many of the big voluntary societies run financial schemes to support lone parents, helping them to stay at home and care for their own children as an alternative to those children being taken into a nursery. There's no harm in asking.

Communes are only for certain sharing people, but can very often suit a one-parent very well indeed. Some communes are religious, some folksey, some curative, some pure hippy, and some just big families without any given aim. Most conduct their finances on a central payment basis: wages may be pooled, domestic jobs almost certainly are allocated. One or two run farms successfully and maintain a self-providing line. If you're gregarious, conscious of needing what the welfare people call 'support' and do not possess a dedicated *personal* philosophy, then you may get on all right. The children almost certainly will love it. Contrary to the general impression, a communal life isn't 'free' and I'm not talking about money. If anything, a fairly sizeable slice of freedom has to be given up in order to get along, wholly, with a close-living group.

Extended families are smaller, usually less self-supporting than full-blown communes. Often they are more altruistically orientated than are larger groups. Many registered foster homes are happy to accept mothers and children, temporarily, between placements of children 'in care'. Extended families seem to function on the grapevine system and Social Service offices can provide useful pointers. There is, however, no central bureau through which these open-hearted families may be contacted; one simply has to ask around. Try, too, the one-parent organizations or, for more permanent membership of such a group, advertise in one of the publications aimed at the less conventional, less conservative, section of society.

'Neighbourhood' is as essential as oxygen to some: those who need an assurance-booster, a cushioning by the old 'street community' such as families two generations back took for granted; borrowing the cup of flour; swapping old wives' tales; minding one another's children. All wholesome and human and urban.

Don't run away with the idea that any present-day support-environment is alien to town living. I may emphasize the bliss of an unencumbered skyline and bare-feet-on-the-grass, but I really do realize that rather more Linears live in built-up areas than out among the daisies. What's more, they choose the pressure, noise and laden air for their own good reasons in preference to what, on the face of it, appears best for them. This deserves attention and analysis.

Obviously town life is not without its advantages. Nor need self-help be confined to country circles. Several urban and suburban families have already amalgamated, and it is a pattern that might be popularized. One shares washing machine, telly, telephone, car, playroom and larger toys. This cutting down on *individual* big-item expenses – not to mention the invisible licences and so on – can boost a one-parent's social rating up from grey E-minus to rosy pink B-plus. You needn't even live in the same house as the others: three terraced homes adjoining would serve as nucleus or three-to-four flats within the same block. Cast about for like minds and get moving.

A Birmingham mother-alone writes, 'I know we're pretty cramped here, but staying where I am does away with having to make new friends. It's a time when – being the sort of person I am – there's a craving for so much human contact. It's necessary for me to be able to drop in on neighbours and relations. I want to unburden myself, to talk out problems. This way I carry on with at least part of my life "the same". The same acquaintances. I know my way about too, and carry on with the same welfare worker. So though my own personal circumstances have changed plenty, my externals haven't.'

She sums up the point of view very neatly. She's not the only parent to stress a need for neighbourly support as well as that of aunts, cousins, and grandparents. And having this ready-made human network of interested people helps with baby-sitting and child-minding.

But of course not all town-based single parents are part of a close and consanguineous group. On the contrary, many feel obliged to move away to another (but similar) area when domestic upheaval strikes ... a new area which offers service and support (perhaps essentially *im*personal support) and a familiar lifestyle.

Arguments for remaining in town run thus:

Day nurseries (as opposed to play-groups and nursery *schools*) are *only* available in towns and suburbs, where numbers of working parents justify the provision of flexible care.

Organized *after-school and holiday provisions* are more likely to exist for older children. *No* rural primary schools stay open after hours or during holidays whereas *some* urban ones do (particularly ILEA).

Play centres, and such as the London parks' 'One O'Clock' clubs, which are supervised by recognized play leaders, are the prerogative of town children. These are preferable, many parents think, to the unsupervised 'rec' on the outskirts of the village.

Youth groups, as well as clubs for younger children, are both more varied and more accessible. A child's individual interests and enthusiasms may be the better explored (of course there are exceptions: wild birds, fossil-hunting, breeding rabbits). Many museums run after-school Saturday morning and holiday schemes. Town libraries, too, offer much to users of the Junior Section, including various activities and story-telling sessions during holidays and after school hours.

Family outings, birthday treats and so on are perhaps cheaper to achieve. There are fewer travel complications (or expenses), less necessity for meals out, exhibitions, theatres (all children love sitting in the 'gods'), shows of all kinds, many of which are free (BBC recorded programmes for instance, TV and radio – apply Ticket Unit).

Also there are advantages for parents. First of all the chances of physical and mental isolation are lessened. Friendship, sometimes geared specifically to the Linear is, if not actually at the end of the street, at the most but a bus ride away. I mean oases like local Gingerbread, evening classes, Mothers' Clubs (springing up everywhere, sometimes run by clinics, churches, 'The Welfare'). And in more and more areas you'll find special Second Start courses being run (see Appendix). These courses aim to familiarize new one-parents with the services open to them, plus providing an insight into such problems as filling in Tax Returns, making legal inquiries, avoiding emotional or social pitfalls.

Shopping, most town parents agree, is on the whole cheaper because of the opportunity to 'shop around' and because of competition between cut-price supermarkets. There's also a better chance of either locating – or starting up – a communal buy-bulk group. Community shops operate in some areas where estates run co-operative buying schemes and sell at small-profit levels. Most new estates are, anyway, built with more foresight than hitherto as planners have woken up to the need for community and convenience.

Transport is easier and less expensive. Every town parent is within reasonable distance of some sort of bus/train service. The country parent, alas, sometimes has to have a car if she ever wants to emerge.

But most of all, perhaps, the urban one-parent is grateful for the proximity of *specialized help*, of a listening ear which is, literally, at the end of a local telephone call. This in itself acts as a terrific reassurance, perhaps even deters its use, for if you know salvation's more or less round the corner you'll often manage to cope without calling upon it.

Further reading

Guide to the Rights of Battered Women, published by SHAC. Free.

Guide to the Rights of the Homeless, published by SHAC. Free.

Guide to New Town Housing, published by SHAC. Free.

Notice to Quit, a leaflet produced by the Department of the Environment. From HMSO or pick it up at any housing advice centre. Free.

Regulated Tenancies, a booklet published by the Department of the Environment. From HMSO or Housing Office. Free.

Rights Guide for Home Owners, published by SHAC at 6op.

Directory of Short-Stay Accommodation, published by National Council for One Parent Families, 225 Kentish Town Road, London NW5 2LX. 65p.

See Appendix

Church of England Children's Society

CAB

Family First

Gingerbread

Housing Corporation

Life

National Children's Home

National Council for One Parent Families

National Women's Aid

Richmond Churches Housing Trust

Salvation Army

Second Start

SHAC

Singlehanded

Social Responsibility Council

Vineyard Project

5 Money

One in six fatherless/motherless children depend totally upon state support, compared to one in 500 two-parented children. Seventy-seven per cent of one-parented children claim free school dinners, compared to eight per cent of two-parented children.

Is there any need to list further comparisons in order to underline the fact that one-parent families are almost always poor – financially, that is?

Personally, I have always tried to ignore money, the acknowledged root of much nastiness. Through all my one-parent years I have perfected, not always through dire need and often with shamefully smug delight, dodges, shortcuts, makeshifts and harmless deprivations which result in lessening the use of it. Yet I am aware that my passion for self-sufficiency and my ingenuity in bringing up my considerable brood on half the quota labelled as official poverty line might not be everybody's shining goal. Cash, however deep I might choose to bury my long neck in the sand, is essential to today's functioning – and tomorrow's. Not everyone is as fortunate as I, with a vegetable plot, goats, fowls and a stringy constitution fit to deal with them adequately. It's no use my nagging selfishly on about planting parsnips and bottling plums when thousands of Linear families live in flats, rooms, or gardenless houses.

Money, then, is a must: and it comes in several ways.

Maintenance from a husband, ex or actual, is often the first thought. For couples with the luck to remain on friendly terms, though separated, it may be possible to come to an agreement informally without rows, or dealing, or begging. However, be wise enough to formalize this agreement while the climate remains equable, even though divorce proper may not, in the early stages, be contemplated. Be sure to separate this maintenance into that which is considered your own keep and that which is considered to be the children's. You can consult a solicitor jointly on this sort of arrangement, but see that you each receive copies of all relevant documents and correspondence. You never know, these may be needed later on. Payment of this type of non-combative maintenance is either made direct by cash or cheque, through a solicitor or funnelled by standing order into the mother's bank account.

Such a private agreement in respect of maintenance can be enforced by the courts, just like any other written contract.

It is pointless to try for maintenance if the man is out of work, or a spasmodic earner, or is out of the country, on a long stay in hospital, in prison, or, indeed, if he is in low-paid employment. It must be acknowledged, and accepted, that blood cannot be got from a stone. There are other means by which we may survive.

Maintenance drawn on sufferance is invariably laced with sourness and certain distress. The quicker it is legally arranged the better – yet the law does seem to take an awful long time. The preparation, often fraught with other problems brought on by the break-up of a marriage, can be harrowing.

One's own idea of maintenance and that of one's solicitor may be oceans apart: not all of us want to draw every last drop we're fundamentally entitled to. Some of us don't want the money at all because any further association, even at one remove, is a recurring reminder of a relationship we need to be allowed to forget. Many solicitors/social workers/advisers of all dyes fail to comprehend how difficult, even repugnant, it is to be forced to receive money from an ex-partner. The whole tenor of society tends to urge us on into the realms of vindictiveness, as though nothing else matters but getting our kilo of flesh. On the other hand I suppose it's part, at least, of the solicitor's job to pursue the tangible on our behalf. Indeed I have experience of a solicitor promoting such zeal that he overrode his own client's conscience-ridden protest and secured an allowance not only for the children of the marriage, but also for the wife's child by another man. This particular mother, unable to bring herself to use the money, burned the cheques as they came in. She was not mad: she was not particularly unusual in her feelings. Her ex-husband had not wanted to subscribe to the children's keep: she had not wanted to accept money from him, especially in the case of her independent child, but the very flow of law had somehow engulfed them in this charade which can be best described as 'solicitors' excitement'. Ultimately she took the matter to court behind her lawyer's back and had the order revoked: she preferred to work her fingers to the bone to earn a one-sided living than buy bread with money ungraciously given. So please, any chance reader who might also be a member of the legal profession, do realize that some women cannot accept money from a man they may well have reason to fear/loathe/despise/pity – there may be an absolutely imperative need to sever all connection. Poverty, here, is a self-imposed predicament.

Maintenance cases are generally heard in the Magistrates' Court, often, alas, involving men who are far from able to provide adequately for their children, let alone the mothers of their children. Cases brought about as ancillary to the action proper may be heard 'in chambers' – rather like a board room – and are not very frightening. It appears that all judges (all I've met) speak extremely softly, gusts of audible words alternate with the inaudible. Purposely, it seems, one is positioned furthest away from the man, and so is perplexed and straining one's ears. It is taken for granted that one only speaks if spoken to.

The average maintenance total for all children works out at around one-fifth of the man's net income. Whether you are deemed eligible for a sum for yourself is a debatable point. Much rests upon your ability to conjure up independent income, your work-power, conduct during the married years and the reasons behind the break-up (whether you left him or he left you, for instance). An allowance for the children's keep is – as long as it is sought and as long as it can be met – their right, regardless of your own personal indiscretions. Often, however, the fight for maintenance is not worth the personal wear-and-tear.

Once the order has been made there exists, oddly, only a sort of gentleman's agreement to pay it.

But what if he doesn't pay up? Or stops pay after a little while? Or remembers some months and forgets others? Then the whole thing goes back to your solicitor, to another hearing 'in chambers' and most likely to something called an *Attachment of Earnings Order*. This means that the money is deducted from his salary at source (rendering this domestic argument public property in the accounts department) and paid to you through your nearest County Court. You will receive a cheque and payment slip every month. Keep this slip. Keep everything. Maintenance can also arrive via the DHSS, which is dealt with further on.

There is nothing compulsory by the way, about attending these subsequent hearings. If you live miles away and have no fears of anything blowing up to your gross disadvantage, then I'd save the cost of train fare and baby-sitter.

Maintenance for an ex-wife goes on for life (his life or hers) unless she either marries again or sets up house with a man who keeps her. Maintenance for children continues until they are of school-leaving age or later if they go on to further education. They don't receive anything after starting a paid, full-time job. If, however, your ex-husband dies before the child's eighteenth birthday, then you may claim a *Child's Special Allowance* from the Department of Health and Social Security. You must apply for this within three months of the father's death. This grant automatically ceases if you re-marry (whereas the natural father's allowance would not have done, had he lived).

Women who were not – and still are not – married to the fathers of their children cannot expect the man to pay personal maintenance, though the children are eligible for support by way of *Affiliation Order* and Social Services and DHSS officers can be very helpful in paving the way. The DHSS will, after all, probably have to make up the difference if you don't put in for rescue money.

It may be difficult to extract acknowledgement of paternity and, in the main, it's his word against yours if you're now on coolish terms. If he's parted with money 'for your support' at any time either during your pregnancy or after the child's birth, then this is taken as fair token of vested interest. At a push it may come to a blood test (his and the child's: a painless and uncomplicated process) which, though not positively proving that he *is* the father, can prove conclusively that he's *not*. The father's contribution comes through in the same way as straight maintenance from a husband, either through the court (if by Attachment Order) or through your bank, in the form of a cheque, or cash direct from the man himself if the arrangement is friendly.

But remember, nobody can force you to put in for an Affiliation Order. Like divorced/separated wives, many single mothers can't bring themselves to extend the begging bowl. Some feel they don't want to risk spoiling their independence. Others quite simply have no wish to share their child, however tenuously. Application for an *Affiliation Order* may be made to the Magistrate's Court, but only by a single or divorced woman, or by a widow. No married woman with an illegitimate baby may apply unless she can prove that her husband isn't the child's father and that she has lost all expectation of being financially kept by him. Any application for maintenance must be made within a year of the baby's birth if no support has ever been offered, or any time up to the child's thirteenth birthday if voluntary payments have been received in the past.

An Affiliation Order requires funds to be paid out until the child finishes his education. An older child may himself apply for an extension order to cover a university or training course if his mother dies.

Maintenance orders, whether from ex-husbands or ex-lovers can always be increased or reduced at the request of one or both parents. It may be wise to ask for a small amount of maintenance initially merely as a safeguard against possible hard times when you might want to enlarge upon it. The general toll brought about by inflation may get you after all.

If the father himself falls upon those same hard times, gets ill, loses his job or his stability, then he (or you) ought to contact the court whence payments come. If his penury is genuine he'll most likely be relieved of his obligations towards you and the children for the time being, and the DHSS will take over.

Men are still sent to prison for non-payment of children's maintenance: an impractical exercise, often resulting in loss of employment which renders all hope of 'catching up' impossible. It's been estimated that around forty per cent of all fathers are behind with maintenance payments at any one time. Certainly a friend of mine who recently spent a year in prison reports that he met dozens of otherwise honest, upright men who were doing time for no more than arrears in that respect.

Some women, through their solicitors, put in for a *lump sum* in lieu of monthly maintenance by Affiliation Order. This, invested, provides an income for the child indefinitely. It's not a bad idea if the man has that sort of money to part with. From his side of the bargain it's a useful way of getting the matter behind him for good. It is excellent for affluent married men who need to keep knowledge of the existence of a spare child from their wives.

The lump sum idea may also be applied to husband/wife/children on the break-up of a marriage. This could result in a lower or non-existent rate of monthly allowance set against the proffered investments, a straight gift of the matrimonial home or school fees. A solicitor's advice should be sought about such arrangements, but obviously it is only practicable when the man has more money than the majority of people.

Social Security this can be claimed by any single-parent in Britain who is genuinely on her uppers. It can either provide the whole and sole income, or top it up after maintenance and wages earned. State bounty comes in many guises and it is infinitely puzzling to find out which offshoots of the main apply to your particular case.

As a parent at home with the children you are entitled to weigh up the pros and cons of paid work. You are eligible for benefits right up to the time when the youngest child leaves school. In fact very few mothers see the whole stretch of their offspring's childhood through while resting 'on the dole'. For, year after year, what started off as life's-blood becomes destructive. The world does not actually owe anyone a living – except the very young, the very old and the very sick – and to imagine that it does is part of the negative plunge into the abyss.

With rare exceptions all new mothers probably want to be intimately involved in the physical care and mental stimulation of their babies. If you're a single-parent with a newborn child then the chances are that you've made a pretty thorough evaluation of your own case. You have come down against adoption, fostering, giving him to Grandma, and may feel strongly in favour of breastfeeding. There should be no guilt whatsoever about your parallel decision to opt for Social Security. If you've already been drawing *Maternity Allowance* through the latter part of your pregnancy, then this will simply be adjusted upwards after the baby's birth.

It's been proved again and again that babies who have experienced early care from their own mothers (or, for that matter, loving care from a *total* mother substitute), retain a balanced attitude far in excess of those who've been moved from woman to woman, from cradle to cradle. Continuity is the thing. Live on a state allowance if you have no hope of other income during this vital stage; and never let your ear incline towards those perennial grumblers who maintain that they pay taxes solely to support scroungers. By giving your child a close mother-baby start, you'll be near to guaranteeing that he'll keep off state-aided tributaries later on. Child Guidance advisers, educational psychologists, social workers of every shape and flavour are at this moment struggling over children who suffered muddles in early life. Public money is being spent in huge amounts on hang-ups triggered off by infantile traumas. Tell that to anyone who implies you're 'scrounging'. The single-parent family works well and in the long run to the advantage of the state, on this pay-now-buy-later system. If you feel bad about it, is there any reason why you have to broadcast the fact? You can even arrange to cash your orders at a distant post office. For all anyone knows you might have a private income.

How to apply for Social Security? You find the address of your local office (every reasonable-sized place has one and country villages are covered by the nearest one; cities and large towns are divided into areas) either in the Post Office, Public Library (notice board or reference section), Town Hall, Social Services office, clinic, doctors' surgery or by looking it up in the telephone directory under Health and Social Security, Department of. Also, leaflets telling how to claim can be picked up at most Post Offices, Job Centres or DHSS offices.

The weekly allowance provides a given basic sum for yourself and for the needs of each dependent child, plus rent, rates and possibly a pittance towards repairs and house insurance. If you're in a mortgaged house the DHSS will pay the interest, though they may justly quibble if the deeds suggest that your ex-husband is sole legal owner. So if he leaves home and stops paying mortgage repayments you must, somehow, pay them yourself or be faced with possible eviction. Take heart, though: time is required for any building society to get possession of a house, and if you act promptly you'll be receiving maintenance or an allowance from Social Security before any movement is made. In any case, it's only fair to write to the building society as soon as you're pitched into one-parenthood and let them know the position.

The machinery of the DHSS often spends a fortnight revving-up preparatory to motion, so if you're getting to the end of your running-away-money don't waste any time before making an application. If hollow with hunger ask for an immediate *Emergency Payment*. Insist upon it. This can be handed out before the red tape process of formal application is gone through. It's best to visit the DHSS office in person (ring to make an appointment if you don't want to wait and wait), but if it really is too difficult or complicated to get there then they will send someone to interview you at home. Do not clean up, wash-up, change into your latest hand-me-down, wipe the child's face or attempt to stop the baby from indulging in his usual afternoon yell. Do not, in short, do anything which might suggest to the visitor that you can cope. Similarly, don't let on that intelligence lurks beneath your unkempt mop; hide Proust and the Romantic Poets, tune to Radio One and practise keeping your mouth a little ajar. For once, with five children, no furniture, and only nine pounds between me and the Great Divide, I was not regarded as a candidate for help. In my naïvety I'd put on a brave face, spoken of possible farm work to which I could take my children, eulogized the value of lentils and marrow bones – generally given the impression that Bossy Bags could manage whatever the storm – and got nowhere.

This attitude is probably unfair and ought not to be taken as a generalization because I suspect that the great majority of Social Security officers are sympathetic and largely human. Others are not. Young, middle-aged, male, female, you never know quite who you're going to get, but, having been allocated an officer, then you're likely to continue with the same one. It is your right, however, to ask for another if character clashes grow bad enough to disturb your sleep. So long as you live at home, physically caring for a dependent child, then you cannot be told to get up and go out to work. Indeed we are the only category of fit people under retirement age who are not required to sign on for employment.

If a wife qualifies for Social Security *in addition to* maintenance her husband's contribution can be paid direct to the

Social Security Office. This is sensible because if his payments fall in arrears she still receives the full allowance each week, just as though his contribution had come through. The Social Security Office is then responsible for chasing up his payments. Useful for parents who aren't very good at arguing or standing up for themselves, or who are simply pressed for time owing to work/house/child-care/lack of transport.

To bring this system about, a wife simply requests the Clerk of the Magistrates' Court responsible for her allowance to send the weekly cheque direct to the Social Security office instead of to her.

Child Benefit is available for every parent who actually has the responsibility for the physical care of a child under sixteen, or nineteen if still at school/college. A claim form is issued at the time of registering the child's birth, or, if the child comes into your care after initial fostering or residential care for which you haven't been contributing, then collect a claim form from the DHSS.

Unsupported one-parent families are eligible for extra child benefit. This is drawn at your Post Office each month, on a separate order book from the one issued for the weekly allowance.

If you become a single-parent, or if regular maintenance for any reason ceases, apply for this additional *Child Benefit Increase* through the DHSS.

Family Income Supplement is for all parents in full-time work (at least forty hours per week) but earning a wage too low to live on. FIS makes up the difference between not enough and just enough. There are leaflets at Post Offices about application.

Incidentally, one-parent families receive the same amount of supplement as do two-parent families; perhaps the only handout by which we do better, head for head, than in a conventional Triangular family.

Any widow whose husband has paid National Insurance for at least three years is entitled to a *Widow's Allowance*. She claims by filling in the form on his Death Certificate and sending it to the DHSS. She'll receive a basic allowance for herself and for each dependent child. This initial allowance lasts for twenty-six weeks which is generally time enough to sort out her late husband's financial affairs. After that, if any children are still under nineteen, she may apply for a *Widowed Mother's Allowance*. She can add as much as she likes by her own earnings (unlike the unmarried or divorced mother who is subject to an earnings block). If she isn't able to go out to work, and the Widow's and Widowed Mother's Allowance isn't decently sufficient, then she must claim additional support through Supplementary Benefit.

All parents actually surviving only by courtesy of Social Security are automatically entitled to various peripheral benefits.

Any family living below Supplementary Benefit level, or at it, even though the parent be in full-time work, may also claim exemption from certain National Health and other payments, though in this case the exemption isn't exactly automatic. You have to ask and then allow for snail-action before the requested rebate or sanction arrives. I once waited three months for a chit authorizing honorary NHS spectacles.

Bargains include exemption from *prescription charges* (no child under sixteen pays anyway, whatever your level of income).

Milk and vitamin tablets are free for expectant mothers and children under five. All children at play or nursery schools receive this milk bounty as a matter of course, regardless of income.

No charge is made by *dentists or opticians*. Obviously you won't get gold teeth or John Denver spectacles, though the NHS standard glasses and teeth are not as awful as people would have us think. Don't, however, expect your dentist or optician to divine your financial status as though by instinct. Ask him for an exemption-from-payment form, which is known as FI.

School meals can be free. Apply to the County or Borough Education Committee. Every child attending any state school should be given a form to bring home at least once a year. Most school meals are well balanced and good to eat, whatever the children may say to the contrary. My own, ranging from junior school to sixth form, report that no discrimination is made between those who pay and those who don't; that, indeed, there's no necessity for others in the class to know they're on the free list. But beware, schools vary; do some personal sleuthing and don't be afraid of making a fuss if there is any obvious singling out. Mine once went to a place where Free Dinner children not only waited in a different queue for their food, but sat at a different table too.

You can claim fares to and from essential hospital visits (outpatients and/or special clinics and possibly reimbursement of fares for visiting *very* close relatives who are on a longish-stay in hospitals). For this see leaflet H 11 about *travel* claims from the Post Office or the DHSS.

Contraception advice, gadgets and pills are free from all NHS Family Planning Clinics. Free, too, from most GPs.

An Extra Heating Allowance is claimable through the DHSS for parents with unusually cold/draughty houses, or who are obliged to use expensive central or electric heating because, for instance, they live in a smoke-free zone. Those who are themselves in poor health, or whose children are in poor health (a bronchitic or asthmatic child), may also be eligible. Ask, don't freeze.

Those on Supplementary Benefit are also eligible for part of their gargantuan electricity bill to be met. Unfairly, to my mind, those of us who in spite of working and patching still fall abysmally below the so-called poverty-line, are ineligible for help with electricity. This is a point we would do well to fuss about.

A Special Diet Allowance can be drawn by those on SB who have to cope with a diabetic, coeliac or other diet which necessitates buying less of the cheap carbohydrate foods, more of the costly protein/fat foods. Ask at the DHSS for this.

A Clothing Allowance for schoolchildren is available for age eleven and again at fourteen. This usually comes in the form of a chit to be spent at a given store, and only on school uniform, underclothing or shoes. Apply to the Education Department. Again, a note about this clothing concession should be sent home from school with your child as the appropriate years come up.

Teenagers' Maintenance Allowances are for families with low incomes for any child who stays on at school after his sixteenth birthday. The amount varies from mean to generous county by county. Apply to the local Education Department as soon as you know that your fifth-former intends staying on in the sixth.

Help from the DHSS may also be obtained for essential *hire-purchase* commitments or for *household equipment* which is desperately needed (bedding, cooking utensils, certain pieces of furniture) and for urgent clothing or footwear.

If you have a handicapped child in the family (mentally or physically) then you may be eligible for a full (day and night) or half (day only) *Attendance Allowance*. Or, if that child is unable to get about under his own steam, you may be able to get a *Mobility Allowance*. Application should be made to the DHSS irrespective of whether or not you draw SB. This is one of the few benefits available for foster children, who are otherwise generally deemed 'cared for' by their maintenance allowance, irrespective of family income level.

Some of the larger voluntary societies are able to give either direct financial or material help to one-parent families who haven't been able to elicit any help through the usual channels. It may be in the form of grants, loans, or clothing. Good in times of crisis. Apply direct.

Most low-income families are eligible for at least some of the available assistance, whether they claim Supplementary Benefit or not. But nothing comes unless you ask.

Further reading

Family Benefits and Pensions (Leaflet FB1), issued by DHSS, free. If unable to locate this invaluable booklet at your Post Office write to Information Division Leaflets Unit, Block 4, Government Buildings, Honeypot Lane, Stanmore, Middlesex HA7 1AY.

See Appendix

Buttle Trust

Child Poverty Action Group

CAB

Citizens' Rights

Cruse

DHSS (and Supplementary Benefits Commission)

Dr Barnardo's

Family Fund

Fifth Demand Group

Gingerbread

National Council for One Parent Families

Rights of Women

Sailors' Children's Society

6 Work

Over a quarter of all Linear parents work full-time. Considering the difficulty in finding jobs to fit in with school hours/holidays, and the grossly inadequate provision of all types of economical day-care, this is in itself pretty remarkable. It destroys too, rather convincingly, the notion that lone parents sit about waiting for the ravens to feed them. Add to these full-timers as many again in part-time work or self-employment and we get a picture of quite formidable independence in the face of seemingly insurmountable problems. The actuality of working, quite apart from the necessity of gathering in loot, restores self-confidence no end. Buying Weetabix with money you've earned by sweat is altogether a different experience from buying breakfast with the outcome of a cashed benefit voucher. Toil, then, is good for us.

Confidence and cash may be the prime motivation, but there are other advantages which follow along the way – the social one for a start. We meet people. Not as pie as it sounds ('Join a club,' urges the advice columnist), for the single parent gets out seldom enough. Work is also splendid medicine for keeping the brain alive (even manual work), so even if we don't land a strictly intellectual job the very difference in routine and physical movement, surroundings and colleagues, does wonders for 'taking us out of ourselves'. Which means, in a way, that we become more interesting and interested people and more interesting parents. Nobody is ever obliged to make an unvarying meal of maternity and domesticity, nor to isolate their little warm world of children-plus-self in a hermetically sealed box. That particular type of restricted situation leads almost inevitably to self-satisfied boredom and inertia which is essentially destructive.

Of course I know work is not always possible because of practical barriers; not always actually desirable (particularly when babies are very small), but ultimately, when basic stability has been attained, it's terrific to prove oneself capable of running one's own show.

The majority of single-parents are in manual, semi-skilled or unskilled employment, even those who possess qualifications worthy of higher things. The simple explanation lies in the fine margins of school hours, for these don't and can't fit in with standard professional employment, with standard office time-keeping.

School hours, as everybody knows, are:

Infants and Juniors 9.00 to 3.30
Secondary Pupils 9.00 to 4.00

There are school holidays too. Three weeks at Christmas and Easter; six weeks or more from the end of July to early September. There are also half-term breaks (usually five to seven days) and occasional days off. Not to mention measles, coughs, visits to the dentist and out-patients.

In a nutshell, we are up against it: limited job opportunities, the probability of far from esoteric employment when we do find it, and the near-certainty of pay matched to the low level of work we are forced to take. Graduates charring, trained nurses working as barmaids, a chemist collecting kelp from Scottish beaches for the fertilizer factory: it happens, and we must be prepared to come down a peg or two until the Big Chance occurs. As it will.

But take note. Any parent existing on Social Security is limited to a certain earnings maximum, above which benefit is reduced pound for pound. This rule leads low-paid people direct to what's known as The Poverty Trap – that abyss out of which it is impossible to climb by working either harder or longer. So for heaven's sake look carefully at your accounts before accepting a really poorly paid job. You may be financially better off *not* working in that particular slot. Ask the DHSS office for the current earnings level.

Full-time jobs are from 9.30 to 5.30 as a rule. Take a long think before you leap. Will you really be able to stand it? Children, house and eight hours' work a day? The ultimate in multiplying one person's energy into two persons' output. Clearly one in four of us does feel adequate to it. So present yourself as available to employers, and decide whether or not you're going to volunteer information about the existence of children. There are two schools of thought. Some people think it better not to tell unless you're asked point-blank. Certainly the bias against single-parents exists in the minds of employers. Can we be relied upon to turn up regularly? Will we find the job incompatible with home ties and throw it up within a few months? In a way these doubts are justified. Thus, before the interview, have your answers ready for the following questions:

(a) Have adequate and reliable day-care arrangements been made for the children?
(b) If, as they will be, children are ill or otherwise obliged to stay at home on a working day, who will stand in at Home? Holidays and half-term too?
(c) Are you likely to be able to bear the physical and mental burden of holding down a full-time job combined with carrying out the normal duties of mother/housewife/laundress/cook/bottlewasher? (Yes, you say, beaming, looking the picture of ruddy good health, assuring the man that your inconvenient flat is all easy-care, drip dry.)

As in almost every other area of life help can be found if you're prepared to look hard enough. But even if you haven't got day-care arrangements absolutely in the bag you must never jeopardize the chances of a good job by dithering. Temporary lying is sometimes most necessary. If the art is new to you, practise.

Yes, you say – again – you run an absolutely foolproof scheme with a neighbour or two so that a proxy-mother is always available in a crisis. And yes, yes, yes, the child is with a registered daily-minder and/or enjoys homely supervision throughout that vacuum between the end of school and six o'clock (now see also chapter 7).

Honestly, lots of jobs are lost because of vagueness over child-care. Just recently for instance I was turned down for a night-assistant post in an old folks' home because the matron had doubts about three great strong teenagers being left in charge of ten- and five-year-old boys between the sleeping hours of 10 p.m. and 8 a.m. I knew that I could cope with the job but she reckoned I couldn't. I wonder, had I rephrased my care arrangements by intimating that an 'adult relative' (my nineteen-year-old son) was living with us, would I then have landed the job?

If you have any qualifications or worthwhile experience it's best to stick to that line – both from the point of view of satisfaction and of pay. However, it's not always that easy. For one thing, and it's an important thing, now that you're a one-parent I doubt whether you can afford private transport, so work must be tailored to a given geographical area. Easy walking or bicycling distance for preference. Public transport is expensive so avoid it where you can. Professional organizations connected with your career can often be more helpful than Job Centres in giving leads to understanding employers.

School work is the single-parents' dreams as it gives you the same hours, same holidays, with matching gaps for measles and flu. And this needn't necessarily mean teaching. Day schools need somebody – preferably with a SRN or SEN certificate – for the medical room. Domestic and kitchen posts are in a state of constant turn-over if you're after using brawn rather than brain. Private schools are still allowed to employ non-qualified staff as assistant teachers (mostly for such as housecraft, needlework, art, and back-up tuition). There's never any harm in contacting a local school in respect of employment, even if they're not currently advertising. Many would be glad to know you're there should their need arise.

Or what about being a lollipop-person at school crossings?

House-matroning or similar at boarding schools is a tolerable way in to the self-support system if you possess a tidy nature and can extend yourself enough to become part of a fairly disciplined community. This is normally open only to mothers with school-age children. It is worth thinking about for anyone springing off into the Linear with neither job nor roof. Scholastic agencies can usually come up with something, more certainly if you have experience or even vaguely relevant training.

Hostels, training colleges, residential establishments of every hue (except perhaps HM Prisons) offer, from time to time, full employment plus a flat or large bed-sitter. Private families do too, though I wish advertisers would find an alternative to that seemingly luke-warm addendum 'child not objected to'.

Eight hours' daily work under the auspices of the National Health Service is almost free for the asking. If there's a hospital within easy reach make inquiries about care facilities for staff children. More of them than you'd think run private crèches for employees' infants. Many allow older children to join the little ones after school. Even if you're not qualified for a remotely nursey job don't be put off; hospitals need people for lesser positions too, and the pay is reasonable-to-good.

Jobs with perks attached – particularly food perks – are much sought after by one-parents with children with voracious appetites. I know a girl whose cooking job in a city day-centre not only gives her free lunch and tea, but also provides take-home extras such as surplus cooked vegetables, soup, bones and stock. Sometimes this take-away is legal (often it depends upon the social conscience of the supervisor), sometimes not. Anyway, I reckon that good food officially destined for the waste bin is better off secreted in a plastic bag in any poacher's pocket than landing up in the place where it's meant to land. If caught you come to no harm by moralizing over a system of deliberate waste in the face of obvious want.

Part-time can mean any time. Ideally it means 9.30 to 3.00, weekdays only, those inviolate hours when the children are at school, safe, cared for and someone else's responsibility. You are then, without strings, available for legitimate employment. But remember, whatever your career, openings for part-timers are always limited. It may be doubly difficult if you also stipulate school holidays off.

Chances are fair for office workers of all kinds, and much more than fair if you're a competent short-hand/typist. Temporary work (full or part-time) of this vein can be bitten off for as little as a week at a time and pay is above the normal 'permanent' rate. Agencies for temps abound in all city areas and Job Centres will also help.

Lots of single parents take on pub work, which fits in splendidly with both school and morning opening hours. If you're chicken about working in the bar you may be able to labour behind the scenes, perhaps cooking or preparing snacks. Wherever there's a brisk midday trade potential employment lurks. Go in and ask. Likewise cafés, restaurants, hotels. You will undoubtedly get a huge free lunch.

Retail shop work, except for quick-turnover establishments like confectioners' and newsagents', are rarely able to offer useful hours. The same applies to reception, library and telephone-exchange work. Don't waste time pursuing the hard-to-get: just see that the Job Centre has your name for reference and then turn to more catchable part-time areas.

Use the Home Help Service, which reaches out into every square inch of the country. Council-employed and registered, you choose your own hours which is marvellous. By far the greatest number of calls for help are from old people, too frail or incapacitated to cope with their own housework and washing. Many will also be lonely, and you must develop a system of keeping up with the chores while listening to reminiscences and/or complaints. Most satisfactory for the gregarious, this work helps to widen the horizons and compels you to count your blessings. Most old ladies and gentlemen love you to bring a child along sometimes and many a child has gained a 'granny' or 'grandpa' through his mother's home help job. A car is not necessary unless you live in a very rural area; and in all cases travelling time is paid for at full rate. No specific qualifications are asked for, though a fair degree of housewifeliness and calm is useful. Apply to the local Social Services which may also run a Family Aides scheme.

Aides provide practical help for families in order to avoid the need for children being taken into care. You're neither nanny nor home help but rather a working auxiliary mother, tactfully showing a less adequate parent how to cope with budgeting, cooking, cleaning and handling her young. It is often tough work, and no good for perfectionists or those who can't suffer fools gladly. But it's satisfying for the sympathetic and practical person and you can be home for your own children by mid-afternoon. The pay is unbelievably good.

Sometimes the same system is extended to the very old or the very handicapped. The point is to help them to stay in their own surroundings with a mite of independence rather than be moved into residential Homes. No particular qualifications are sought, but you must weigh up your own ability to function in a job where two steps forward can also involve at least one step back.

Evening work is worth thinking about if you have someone to baby-sit (for example a friendly lodger on a reduced rent in lieu). Get the children into bed first, without hurry, without forgetting the story or seeing that the pot's where they can reach it. Then on to barmaiding, factory late-shift, nursing (or ancillary), catering, waitressing, hotel chambermaiding, washing-up, school or office cleaning, cinema or theatre usheretting or doing whatever the employed do at bingo or the dogs. Most of this is physically exhausting and hard on the legs, but lucrative.

Night work is ripe for consideration only if you really do get time to sleep by day. Useless, for instance, if you have pre-school children who don't attend nursery or play-school. Breakfast can present a problem as many shifts don't finish until 8 a.m., time already for the children to be up and getting ready for school. Such nocturnal labouring is probably best for house-sharing one-parents so that a box-and-cox caring system can function. The great pull towards night work is the pay. It's at least one-and-a-half times the day rate because of 'unsocial hours'. There are jobs in hospitals, institutions, night canteens, factories, switchboards. Social Services in many areas run a list of person-sitters who will keep the ill or the very elderly company at night: ask about it. The remuneration is handsome.

Dawn work, which is almost exclusively factory, shop and office cleaning and is restricted to urban areas, is solely for parents who can stand getting up at 5.30 a.m. to join the army of old faithfuls, resting actors and hyperactive housewives who tend to look upon the job as their prerogative. Unsocial hours again, so the pay's good. Look up Industrial and Office Cleaners in the Yellow Pages and dial around: there are always vacancies. You're home again no later than 8.30.

Baby-comes-too jobs are practicable, as far as I can find out, in two lines only. Charring and nannying. And there are reservations on the former, because jolly soon the baby is too old to sit quietly in the pram while mother hoovers and scrubs. On the other hand, many employers are easy about school-agers tagging along during the holidays. Nannying is ideal because you do a full working day without having any frets about your own child. Daily nannies are much in demand by professional parents, who like to have the house to themselves after the day's grind. Training is not always expected, though certain

74

sensible standards are. Job hunt through a domestic agency (no cost to you, that's paid by the employers), or a specialist magazine like *Nursery World*, or the top dogs' newspapers.

Odd jobbery can make you a decent living, honestly. That is, if your standards aren't all that luxurious. Look around you, read the notice-boards, pick the local paper out of the waste bin, and act. Stagger three or four odd jobs and you find yourself with a basic living wage: for instance, I once put in three afternoons a week at the local bookshop, took on a couple of temporary foster-children, coped with the bookings, cleaning and general caretaking of the church hall and managed the lettings of a nearby house while its owners were abroad and was still around to see the children back from school.

If you live in the country there's often casual farm work to be picked up. Hoeing sugarbeet, picking or riddling potatoes, or plucking fowls (especially before Christmas). In fruit-growing areas there's always a need for labour through the summer and autumn. Children of all ages are generally most welcome though they must understand that all machinery is out of bounds. Apply direct to farms.

Working from home is great if you're a fairly cheerful solitary, but death if you can't take your own company undiluted. First, consider whether you could run any sort of business or service on the strength of qualifications already possessed. Hairdressing, chiropody, poodle-clipping, dressmaking, childminding? Lesser 'home work' may conjure up visions of slave labour and the rag trade, hemming up fifty vests for tuppence. Draw a veil over those visions, and if you're ever tempted to take in what's known as 'out-work' be sure to make full inquiries about pay and supply before you get involved. Some manufacturers still echo shades of Dickens, though it's true that most don't. And it's not all sewing either. Manufacturers of industrial components send out items for home assembling. Sports equipment may be brought in for stitching, sticking. Apply boldly at local factories, keep a sharp look out in the local press, or ask at the Job Centre.

Both child-minders and foster parents must be approved by and registered with the local council. Foster-parents receive the statutory maintenance which does not count as earnings as far as the income tax man is concerned, even though the allowance is now fairly generous. Income from child-minding (in the day-time only) is seen as earned income and must be declared. Some boroughs run what they call Day Fostering, a scheme through which needy children get a taste of freedom/homeliness/affection. This is well paid in comparison with free-lance daily-minding because part of the payment is regarded as 'wages'. But you can't pick and choose whom you take; the council does that for you. Certain counties run Special Fostering and pay such a high rate that it makes you catch your breath. This is only for long-term one-parents who have taken all knocks already and survived, for the riches of Special Fostering are earned by taking on problem teenagers who are not just little problems. Another warning while we're still on the subject: don't be tempted to take on private foster-children. Parents without the backing of Social Services can seldom afford to pay the statutory rate, nor have you any redress if payment isn't forthcoming. The risk may be slight, but it exists. And you can't afford to be the loser.

Paying guests If you have a spare room, use it. Even if you haven't and there's a ghastly bill to be paid, move the children in together, or with you, and let their room out for a short period. Paying guests are profitable and are usually out all day. Overseas visitors, particularly summer visitors, fill the coffers fastest. Get on to an approved file at the local tourist bureau or summer school. List the views, places of interest, whether you'll accept dogs or children, do vegetarian catering provide home-made wines or whatever. Lure them in with the off-beat.

Bed-sitter tenants are not fully protected under the *Rent Act 1968*, and the more you provide in the way of services (meals, laundry, cleaning) the less attention will be paid to any lodger's stubborn refusal to quit. However, his stay can be prolonged by up to six months at a time should he choose to take the case to Tribunal. So to be really one hundred per cent certain of impermanent lodgers, recruit only students (write to the Accommodation Officer of any training college, Technical School or University Lodging Bureau), holiday tenants or those employees whose firm itself advertises for rooms (you then have a comeback on the person responsible for placement). Her Majesty's

Stationery Office produces a useful free booklet which you'd do well to get hold of before you launch out into the landlady bracket.

Use accommodation agencies and district newspapers advertising to make yourself known. Always collect the rent in advance, and give a receipt (keep a copy yourself). Also get a deposit against gas and electricity if relevant; you can get a sort of gauge fixed to power sockets to measure the amount used. This is especially useful if the paying guest runs record player, radio, hair-dryer and electric train set, or if you suspect he leaves the heater on all night.

'Ordinary' paying guests may become a bore, or unwanted stickers. They may have problems of their own, or have time on their hands to take up yours. It sounds mean perhaps, but tread carefully. I know one single mother who takes in emergency visitors for the Samaritans, another who takes in ex-prisoners. Both are saints, and as such get no reward in this world. There's also the real danger of being so busy 'doing good' to strangers that the family itself gets a shortage of loving care. Some paying guests do seem to expect a full-time listening ear. Then there's the lady who practises day-starvation followed by wild midnight fryings. So, unless you aren't really in it for the money, better not set about creating your own redemption centre.

Artiness, commercially, can be done on two levels. High and low will earn you pin-money, non-declarable extras, no more. This is the extended hobby which involves little or no financial outlay and little difficulty in marketing so long as your standard of handicraft bears scrutiny. I suggest peg-dolls, hand-knitting, crochet, macramé, patchwork, making shoe/toy/laundry bags or toys of all kinds. Don't be afraid to tout samples round local gift and craft shops. One lone mother rents a market stall every two or three months to sell her output of bean-bag animals and babies' pinafores.

The high level takes in more professional crafts, those which often need initial finance to set up. When really moving this can cannon you into the realms of genuine self-employment and you needn't always have art school training. Most crafts can be learned at evening classes or through a good textbook. Select your line and persevere. Costume jewellery may suggest pictures of heavy rocks on matronly bosoms, but you can improve the image. The tools needed depend upon the medium in which you work, but as little as five pounds can start you off. Costume jewellery sells.

The knitting machine really is an investment if you use it and your commercial know-how in partnership. Most machines can be bought on hire-purchase (allowed for if you use Social Security) and the fullest possible directions are always included. Boutiques will trade with you or orders may be obtained through regional advertising. The several home-knitting mums I've met report that after initial advertising the job keeps itself going through recommendation. One had a three-month waiting list for orders. Wool can be bought cheaply in bulk direct from the mills – you often see it advertised in women's magazines.

Pottery and weaving, tailoring and dressmaking, the manufacture of mobiles and paper decorations, the knitting of children's slippers, bread and cake-making for a health food shop, the painting of nursery friezes to customers' own ideas: all these jobs are tackled by various single parents to the point where the crafts can no longer be regarded as mere hobbies. Don't be afraid to try.

Coaching is for the more academic among us. This doesn't necessarily mean teaching older teenagers who are working for exams. Even primary school children often need coaching in basics. Adults too: especially if you can offer languages. English to foreigners is another ploy: special training is intensive but short. It's good if you're prepared to work out-of-school hours and at weekends. Apply to scholastic agencies or advertise locally. Note that teachers working with pupils on the Adult Literacy Scheme, now functioning in all parts of the country, *don't* get paid.

Typing For perfectionists only. People who farm out their literary babies want a first-class job done. Two-finger typists like myself should think again; though nobody's going to see how fast you go. *Translation* pays handsomely, *indexing* too. Work through commercial agencies, specialist magazines, local advertising. Or for translation and indexing contact publishers or authors' agents direct.

Addressing envelopes, that home-occupation one always hears so much about is, I reckon, a myth. Even if it were not a myth I wouldn't wish it upon my least favourite person: the boredom and non-constructiveness would be death. The only time I've done any mass-addressing of mail was for pre-election matter and that was voluntary.

Be warned off *commission work* too. For every one who lands a profit a hundred must sink without a bubble. Cosmetics, brushes, magazines, encyclopaedias, double-glazing or cavity walling: keep off it, whatever the seemingly foolproof lure. It's three years since I had to buy any washing-up liquid, and that because a friend invested over £50 in bulk purchase on a 'can't fail' pyramid scheme. He was talked into it as soon as, in his mind's eye, he envisaged himself as the millionaire soap-king. He sold a mere dozen bottles. That severe timidity brought about by knocking at strangers' doors was too much for him. And with how many golden bottles left waiting in the attic?

Only one notch up the panic scale is the party-giving line. A few women might make money out of selling plastic boxes as they dish out free coffee and sandwiches; but most don't. Unless you enjoy a gamble leave *party-selling* alone, however tempting the ads.

Telephone-selling is another occupation only to be entertained as a gamble, not if you need money for a cert. This is commission selling again. You ring up poor unsuspecting subscribers and try to persuade them to advertise in a given paper, take advantage of cut-price roof insulation or any other dozen ideas they wouldn't dream of doing off their own bat. A conscience-buster, this. Opportunities for optimistic amoralists in local papers, notice boards, some national papers.

Training or re-training Full-time courses can be difficult to fit in with full-time parenting. Not exactly impossible, but utterly dependent upon reliable and regular day-care. They can also be a drain on mental and physical resources. Ask yourself a few questions before you so much as pen the application form.

Part-time training is best for us, though there's still room to fight for more flexible hours. Some colleges start at 9.00 a.m., for instance, simultaneously with the school bell. Many others are ideal, with 10.00 to 1.00 as set hours. So don't jump at the first course you hear about : pick one to suit both you and the children.

The Training Opportunities Scheme (TOPS) offers around five hundred courses, from secretarial through to heavy goods vehicle driving. Maximum length, one year. Some courses lead to City and Guilds certificate. You are automatically assessed for a grant as soon as your place is approved and dependent children are taken into account. Trainees must be over nineteen but there is no upper age limit.

Teaching is the goal for a good many single parents, and understandably so. The BEd degree course takes three years. There is no upper age limit for admission. Only competition. Student grants are available, plus extra for the support of children. Applications should be made to the college of your first choice, then to the Central Register and Clearing House in the autumn of the year before starting.

For general help over deciding to take training in any field, go to the local Job Centre or area Education Department. Warning: private Career Advisory Services are unbelievably expensive, so steer clear.

Evening classes are limited in range of subject but can serve to open doors into a career. They are good if you share a flat or can be sure of a regular baby-sitter. Most councils responsible for running the classes are willing to let people on Supplementary Benefit enrol for a reduced fee, or for free. Ask.

Correspondence courses might be made for people like us. You work while the child has his nap, while the neighbour takes him for a walk, before he gets up in the morning and/or after he goes to bed at night. These quiet times are essential for concentration. Don't believe stories of women who write theses or learn reams of data with their tiny darlings crawling round the chair making motor-car noises. Iron willpower and determination are other little qualities imperative to the success of home-study so every time you feel yourself flagging make another resolution not to become one of the fifty per cent who give up before qualifying. It's always worth writing to the principal of the correspondence college telling him of your domestic background and financial straits as you may get a reduction. In any case staggered fees are always negotiable.

Courses on dozens of subjects are advertised in the educational columns of national and specialist publications.

Apply to *The Open University* for your BA (three years minimum) or for any one of a hundred non-degree courses (ten months). No qualifications are needed before you enrol, apart from age – you must be twenty-one or over. Some subjects necessitate your having BBC television and/or VHF radio link-ups. There are Study Centres throughout the country for practical help when needed. Applications for all courses should be made between April and October for the following academic year. Grants are available.

Further reading

Rooms to Let, published HMSO. Free.

See Appendix

Cruse
Gingerbread
Job Centres
Liverpool Gingerbread
National Childminding Association
National Council for One Parent Families
National Foster Care Association
New Opportunities
Open University
Singlehanded
TOPS
Vineyard Project

7 Day-care:
nurseries and schools

'I can either be a good conscientious mother and bad bread-winner or a full-time working mum who isn't there when her children need her. There doesn't seem to be any way out.' So writes one woman, echoing the cry of many thousands more: for day-care is destructively inadequate in catering to our needs. To the lone parent the nursery can signify the difference between survival and collapse, between pride and apathy, between a happy home and a squirrel-wheel of anxiety.

Local Authority nursery places provide for just under five-and-a-half of every thousand under-fives, and we can be grateful that one-parent families tend to receive preferential treatment. Not a very cheering statistic, though, for a mother contemplating a return to work. Obviously we must make use of private nurseries and professional 'minders'. We must look, too, at the day-care provided by the large voluntary societies and charities, usually heavily subsidized, making charges of nil to reasonable amounts, unlike the privately run schemes, which can be expensive. Probably the most satisfactory way of over-whelming this great bugbear of the working parent lies, again, with self-help: we must mind one another's children.

Up comes the brick-wall attitude and the mumbled clue: 'economics'. Few parents, it is argued, earn enough to pay a friend to mind the baby. Says one mother, 'The mere £6 isn't nearly enough for taking on the burden (sic) of some-one else's child.' Yet nurseries are not run free, and the great cry is for more of them. And if just under half of us stay at home anyway, looking after our own children, surely non-working parents could be persuaded to look upon the 'burden' as worth while? Somehow we must explode the easy let-out of placidly accepting the status quo.

Gingerbread groups in some areas keep a list of willing minders. Other areas could follow suit. We could also further help ourselves by angling for use of school buildings, halls and so on for after-school and holiday care. Schemes have already been set up in Surrey, with parents and volunteers manning the operation. Pressure must be brought upon Education Authorities to allow us to use premises, but we should begin by firing a bit of enthusiasm amongst ourselves.

Mutual help over part-timing is perhaps the easiest swap to achieve. For a long time I looked after a small boy while his mother worked in a pub during the mornings. She came home, had lunch with us, then took over for the afternoon stint while I went off to be an assistant in a book shop. Neither of us owed the other money: both of us were able to earn a little extra. Get your wants out on the grapevine.

Some get lulled into a false peace by thinking that, once a child reaches his fifth birthday, day-care problems will evaporate. School holidays – Easter, Summer and Christmas – must be faced practically. We cannot all work in the schools themselves: would that we could (there were fifty applicants wanting the post of dinner-lady in a local school recently). Paid help at home can be balanced against income tax (those of us who earn enough to pay any). Synchronize your holidays if you can, though you mustn't exactly expect to get a total of twelve weeks a year. Friendly neighbours, welcoming relatives, summer camps and the like, are all possibilities. But never send a child off to total strangers unless in a dire emergency: meet them once or twice with him, before arranging any day-long visits. Older children are often shy of strangers. They may cover this shyness by showing-off and being generally ghastly, which could put paid to the whole enterprise. Younger children, up to six or seven, have little or no appreciation of time and they may feel abandoned even if left with strangers for a relatively short duration. Prepare them carefully.

If we really do come up against the immovable object then we have to think wholly in terms of the interests of the child – even if it means marking time until we find a job which does recognize the day-care problems of single parents. Your child is more important than any job if he needs you.

Local Authority Day Nurseries are run under the protection of Social Service departments. Most city areas have at least one nursery, accepting children from three months to five years old whose parents live within permitted boundaries. Citizens' Advice Bureaux, Job Centres and reference libraries should keep current information on nurseries. The shocking truth is that over one-quarter of all local authorities provide no nurseries at all.

However, even if you do live in a 'lucky' area, remember that waiting-lists are usually very long. Some mothers put out feelers weeks before the child is born: certainly don't leave it until you're in desperate need of immediate relief. Opening hours are 8.30 a.m. to 6.00 p.m. purposely geared to parents in full-time employment.

A number of corporation nurseries employ a points system when allocating places (most London boroughs and Leeds) and one-parent families come near the top of any list. Charges are statutory, but in some cases Social Services will bend to a grant. If you're in a low-paid job and the nursery fees threaten either to cripple you or cause you to wonder why the blazes you're going out to work at all, get up and take your case to the office. No need to be 'on their books' or ever to have asked for anything before. The Social Services are not merely a soft pad for inadequates, they're there for us to use. Financial help is also available, so just set about making your presence obvious.

By the way, they have the power to pay *private* or *community service* play-group fees as well, but often need persuading to consider those of parents not already known to them. The tack to employ here is the watertight argument concerning the therapeutic value of change. Parents who choose (or are compelled by circumstances) to stay at home with the children must appreciate the stimulation afforded by play-group attendance. It also buys for those parents time for themselves, another necessary ingredient of the happy family.

Precious few infant and primary schools have nursery departments, but some do. These accept children from two-and-a-half to five years. As sub-fives don't officially come under the Education Authorities some charge has to be made, but the same opening to the official begging bowl is available. Sound out the Education or Social Service Departments. This is particularly applicable to the London area.

Private nurseries: 'works' nurseries Both categories must be approved by the council before opening their doors to any child. Thus any nursery you see advertised, whether part of an employment notice or not, must be bona fide. Old biddies

84

who 'love children' can no longer set up in business as and how they please.

Private schemes are unlikely to offer reduced fees in order to ease the lot of the single parent. The principal is in it for the money, for her own livelihood: but remember, as with the part-time play-group, councils might well help financially if funds are really tight.

Hospitals and factories providing child-care facilities have already been touched upon in the last chapter. Some will accept older children during school holidays. Most of these 'works' nurseries are heavily subsidized by the firms (or Area Health Authorities) themselves. This makes sense, for the cut in staff turnover and training is a great bonus, and though the parent is more or less tied to a particular company the advantages are enormous, and day-care fees minimal. From the child's point of view, he is comforted to know that mother is near. From the parent's point of view there is no long daily trek from home to nursery to work, from work to nursery to home. The arrangement suits all.

One electronics firm in Farnborough, Hampshire, runs an eight-week summer play-school for employees' children. The age-range covers the toddler stage up to mid-teenagers and the premises are open full-time. Here one is talking of a contribution towards funds, not a fee. I can't believe that this is a one-off project, for it makes such good sense. Tracking down companies such as this depends upon individual detective work in a given area. Keep your ears open. Ask around. Job Centres should act as pointers too.

Many universities and other training colleges support day-care programmes for students' children. Don't leave it too late: make inquiries when you enrol. Cambridge, Edinburgh and Sussex make definite provision, and other universities must too.

Voluntary societies: charities This is where our needs are really understood, where concern for the children of working single parents is being met with practical help. Not so long ago the big voluntary societies and 'rescue' organizations were solving social problems by actually splitting families, by putting children into Homes. Now they go to great lengths to keep families together: one-parent families too.

Day nurseries (full-time) and play-groups (part-time) run by such as Save the Children Fund and the Salvation Army have gradually multiplied over the years since the bulk of council-run schemes closed down in the period immediately after the last war (when there were actually twice as many nursery places as there are today).

People tend to think that voluntary play-groups are reserved for deprived children. This isn't necessarily so. Lump a whole lot of deprived children together and progress isn't half as swift as with children drawn from various family circumstances. So don't feel that you need be *in extremis* before applying. The broad ambitions, at least of the SCF, are to create conditions in which children can grow to a healthy maturity. Citizens Advice or Social Services would be able to say if there are any schemes in your area. One charity alone runs forty-five nurseries and play-groups in London and another forty-nine in the provinces. As before, lone parents nearly always get priority over others.

Daily-minders, child-minders There seems to be something a trifle archaic about those terms. A touch of the Mrs Gamp perhaps? But be reassured: child-minders come in all varieties and are far from being mere shepherds, otherwise they'd never get their registration. Registration is absolutely essential. It is in fact illegal for a child-minder to ply her trade without it. Be bold enough to ask to see a minder's letter of registration if you have contacted her through hearsay instead of through Social Services. You've a right to know that your child is in capable hands ... and there are an awful lot of unregistered people still in it for pin-money. Beware.

Registered minders are not necessarily trained in child welfare, though a fair proportion are. Married nurses, nursery nurses and teachers, working at home while their own babies are small, are the pick of the list. Try to get one if you can.

Any premises intended for the use of child-minding must be formally inspected by the Area Health Authority. Play space available per head, window area, fire safety, access to public road: all these points and more are taken into consideration before registration is granted. Some authorities are fussier than others. Often it's a case of supply and demand.

Some urban boroughs, particularly in London, do provide a sort of domiciliary training for minders. Visiting play-leaders may take children out to local parks or open spaces. Or the leader may stay in the minder's home for a while, playing constructively with the children while at the same time educating the minder in the principles of play, routine and environmental influence. The Save the Children Fund offers such a service.

It's been estimated (Finer) that one-third of all children placed with registered daily-minders come from single-parent backgrounds. This reiterates the lack of council-backed nurseries which cover these full workday hours most essential to an independently minded parent. If we are hell-bent on supporting ourselves then we must make use of daily-minding, a free-lance system of private infant care, and take pot luck on the charges, which are entirely up to the minder herself. Try the Social Services or one of the voluntary societies if costs are stiff: or one of the few benevolent charities which incline towards cash grants for the needy Linear.

Day Fostering is marginally different from child-minding. It is a phenomenon exclusive to congested areas and generally involves not necessarily working mothers or fathers but parents under stress (with children under stress by a process of osmosis). All children in day fostering are referred by the Social Services and all such foster parents are paid by the council direct. Well paid too (here's a job for the maternal among us). The child's own parent contributes only what she can afford, if anything. This contribution is paid to the council, so that any given foster parent has no idea who's paying full and who's paying nil. This provision is also open to single fathers who are not obliged to be overcome by stress but just expected to use the service as a means of acquiring the freedom to work.

Baby-sitters, within your own home, are your own risk. Unless known to you personally, and known to be capable/kindly/unflappable, it is always wise to ask for the name of a referee you may telephone, preferably another parent for whom he/she has baby-sat. Nobody under the age of sixteen may legally be employed in the care of another human being. Exceptions are only made in cases of baby-sitting for limited hours (a total of eight hours a week – not more than two hours per day during the school term) by children aged fourteen to sixteen. In any case, always be sure to give your baby-sitter the telephone number of wherever you are likely to be for the duration of her sit, or the telephone number of someone else whom she may contact in an emergency. Also a doctor's name and telephone number. If there is no telephone in the house an address of a near neighbour is essential. And make sure that neighbour is going to be at home.

Baby-sitting agencies are generally too expensive for us. If you must get hold of someone from a 'pool' try to use the local PTA or Gingerbread list, or even better, form a reciprocal group of your own.

Aides are a species of high-powered Home Help. Aides come into your home to work either with you or in your absence. The whole idea is based on taking preventive measures, on bolstering up family cohesion as an alternative to children being taken into care. Most especially useful in the case of working lone fathers. They are not available in all areas yet. Inquire at the Social Services department.

After-school and holiday care This is really the most almighty bugbear for the working single parent. One, too, where self-help is most apparent and mainly spurred on by the efforts of local Gingerbread groups. Croydon's 'Gingerbread Corner' is the showpiece, created with enormous determination by single-parents and willing friends. They also had the nerve to ask not for pennies and pounds piecemeal, but for thousands with which to revitalize the shell of the vandalized house and make it a fit place for children to play in after school and during the holidays. Where Urban Aid and the local council couldn't help, the EEC Poverty Programme could – to the tune of £12,000. Magicote gave them paint, British Industrial Sand gave them six tons for the sand-pit, and the army produced an assault net. Begging on such a magnificent scale has to be admired. And sixty one-parent children in Croydon have a safe and stimulating house to go to until Mum or Dad gets home from work. The cost to parents per week is very slender, and the house is available as a meeting-place for Gingerbread parents in the evenings, and may be used for conferences.

Plymouth Gingerbread, encouraged by this excellence, have cooperated with Dr Barnardo's in forming an After-School Care Centre in that city.

The Inner London Education Authority runs a free after-hours scheme in many of its primary schools. These same schools are open for business all day during holidays, when a hot lunch is also provided. Details of these super-schools can be obtained from the ILEA.

Registered minders are often willing to take children for this overlap period: ask for a list at the Social Services. Neighbours or relatives are frequently used, with varying success. Get your needs humming in the neighbourhood. If the PTA has any sort of news-sheet or notice board, utilize it and ask around at the next Gingerbread meeting. Don't just accept that your child must join the *million* others in Britain who go home after school to an empty house. Remember, it can be frightening for a child to be alone indoors; there is always potential danger; neighbours may complain (and not only direct to you, but to such as the NSPCC or Social Services). Don't let yours become a latch-key child.

the Comprehensive system, there are controversial schools and obliged by law to receive full-time education. You don't actually have to send them to school, though most of us do. This gives us space to earn our living, do the chores, make and contain contacts other than those immediately child-orientated. The child also takes this advantage of getting away from us, his hitherto sole pivot. He makes friends, responds to new disciplines and relates to adults other than the monolithic mother (father). All this in addition to straight learning.

Day schools are more-or-less the normal step. About 85 per cent of all children, one-sided or two-sided, attend what are known as the maintained day schools: the state schools. With tough rulings on the catchment theme, our choice of school is – on the face of it – minimal or nil. We all know that, within the Comprehensive system there are controversial schools and good ones. The element of luck rests upon geographical position, but we as single parents are no more morally justified in sending our children to a school of which we do not personally approve than any other set of parents. Never send a child to any school without inspecting it first, even if there appears to be no choice. In fact, if you feel passionately enough about it, there are other facets to the brittle subject of your child's education. And we, lop-sided and impecunious, hold something of a trump card by way of special entry.

Now the rich, we all know, can send their children to private schools and hardly notice the dent in their income. The 'comfortably off' can do so with moderate adjustment, cutting out frills such as second car, holidays abroad, Stilton cheese and new shoes. Below that 'comfortable' income there is seldom any thought of sending any child to join the classes of fifteen instead of the classes of thirty. They just couldn't do it without falling to a level of oatmeal-diet. Yet we, poor though we are, very often *can* achieve the top for our children if we're prepared to stick our necks out.

Many public day schools were founded by philanthropists who inclined towards helping needy children in certain given categories. The Trusts thus established to cover the education of such children still continue to bring in revenue. This income can be set against present-day fees by way of grants. My adopted ten-year-old enjoys a 'privileged' education at private school at one-third of full fees, thanks to a benefactress who lived almost 300 years ago. Often these grants are relevant only to a given locality; in our case we qualified on two points: by living in a certain parish and being in receipt of a somewhat stringent income. Subsidized (or sometimes entirely free) places are usually advertised in the district press at the end of each calendar year, with a view to places being taken up at the beginning of the subsequent September. Ask at your town hall which should hold information on any such local charities. Or, as I did, boldly inquire at any particular school you fancy and try your chances. The *Public School Year Book* or *Annual Charities Digest* are useful references too, both of which should be stocked at your reference library. See also the *Directory of Grant-Making Trusts*.

No matter what type of day schooling we opt for, we must always support our children in their education. A quiet time for home-work is essential, even if we've been assured that TV and general racket are no distraction. They are. An older child may choose to go to the reference library to do homework. Don't be afraid to give intellectual help, and always stimulate his interests. The library service is free so use it. Kindle a good rapport with his teacher. Go to PTA meetings. Be civil to other parents as you may be useful to one another.

Boarding There are recognizable types of 'boarding school child' and unrecognizable ones too. The former are the extroverts, the gregarious kickers of balls who boast a million friends and show strong signs of built-in independence. They may also be the self-confident swotters who have every intention of bettering their lot by way of their brains. If boarding school is mentioned they'll probably jump at the chance.

The more immediately unrecognizable prospective boarders are those with problems, social or emotional. The one-parent child may, for instance, have such a pull of responsibility towards his mother/father that getting away for nine months in the year is his only way of regaining childhood. Oddly enough the 'school phobic' child will frequently opt for boarding rather than stand the *daily* horror of making his way to school.

Between the two groups floats a band of children who fit neither way, yet are perfectly happy about leaving home. We, as single-parents, must always look at their situation in relation to that Linear state. If starting boarding school follows too quickly on the heels of parental separation there is a possibility of the child suffering what he sees as 'double rejection'. Never talk about a child being 'sent away' to school: the term itself reeks of disposal, especially at a time when sensitivities may be raw. If in any doubt on the subject of boarding, don't be afraid to make use of the School Psychiatric Service, which is free and organized through the Social Services or the child's head teacher.

It cannot be denied that, from the working parent's side of the matter, boarding is something to consider seriously for the older child. The freedom to work unrestrictedly for three-quarters of the year is quite something. Single mothers also lose some of the guilt and worry sometimes felt over the child having no male influence.

Boarding is available for almost any child who needs it, or really wants it. The one-parented child is invariably given priority over others where free or subsidized places are concerned. About half the County Education Authorities in Britain run at least one boarding school and those counties who have none are often willing to pay fees for out-of-county boarding. With rare exceptions these schools take children from the age of eleven, so applications should be made (to local Education Departments, not to any school direct) during your child's final year at primary school. The 'less able' are just as eligible as the 'able' – there is no scholarship as such. Interviews are generally held in May for entry the following September. Most schools are small compared to Comprehensives and the majority are co-educational, though there's nothing to stop you requesting a single-sex school if you have reasons.

As an example, Essex runs three boarding schools, two co-educational, one boys only. Each school takes some 200 pupils. Fees, as elsewhere, are graded on parental income and range from nil to full amounts. You must have one whale of an income to be categorized under the latter, which is unlikely in the case of any one of us. Fees in county-run schools cover board only: tuition is always free for all pupils.

Both my older boys went to Fyfield School in Essex where they flourished between the ages of eleven and seventeen. Advantages, they confirm, lie in escaping from the apron-strings, learning independence (not quite synonymous), working with male human beings and 'chatting up birds'. The academic side was adequate and they were almost obscenely well-fed.

We need not stop at county boarding. Scholarships and presentations pepper the public schools like so much manna waiting to be gathered up. 'Disadvantaged' children – a questionable adjective – generally receive special weighting and boys' and girls' schools are equally generous. There are also peripheral gifts: one of my daughters, now in her third free year at a first-rate school, has clothing provided down to the last stitch of navy-blue locknit and shoes as well.

True, scholarships must be won, so there's no point in aching for a grand school if your child isn't at least medium-clever. One single mother writes, 'One advantage in bringing up my children alone is that a good deal less confusion arises as to aims and purposes in life. My husband could never see the need for a girl to have as good an education as possible, leading to financial and practical independence.'

Keep a look out for notices in educational columns of certain publications and, as with the day schools, get hold of a copy of the *Public Schools Year Book* and the other two directories mentioned earlier.

Incidentally, once at school there is no need for other pupils to know that your son/daughter has a free place. This is between the governors and yourself: in most cases the headmaster/mistress is as much in the dark about who pays what as is the great British public. If you feel really twitchy about it, why tell even the child himself? There's no pressing cause.

Education otherwise is the umbrella term given to home-teaching. Not many single parents can afford time to educate their offspring round the dining-room table, though there's nothing illegal about doing so. Indeed, I did this for my first year out of marriage, when the children and I were living in a remote part of Wales with neither transport nor money. The Parents' National Educational Union is the recognized body supporting the home-schoolroom. With enrolment one receives a detailed syllabus, textbooks, guidelines. As long as you stick to these, or otherwise assure the County Education Authority that your child is receiving adequate full-time schooling, nobody can *make* you toe the majority line. The problem is that 'social' objections are apt to be put up as reasons for dis-continuing this domestic-style learning programme. We are made to feel guilty about isolation, mother-ties, lack of a science laboratory. Fight though, if you honestly know you're right.

Talented children There are special scholarships to be won in the fields of music, ballet, and the stage. A few rural counties have farm-schools where agriculture and horticulture play a larger-than-life part in the normal educational curriculum. Local Authorities or specialist professional organizations will be able to supply leads, or refer to those aforementioned direc-tories. Such scholarships usually involve boarding.

Delicate children For children who suffer from asthma, eczema, and more positively permanent disabilities like epilepsy, mental or physical handicap, there are special schools which give special care. Help with fees is always available if your chosen school happens to be in the private sector. Apply to local Health or Education Departments, Save the Children Fund or National Children's Home. Again, the schools are usually boarding.

Disturbed children There are schools for emotionally unsettled children who don't seem amenable to change for the better under home conditions. I'm not talking about the odd bad temper or short-term worry, but about constant aberrations from the norm. If you really feel you can't cope with a problem contact Child Guidance. They are almost inevitably boarding schools, often a good way away from home. Fees would be met by the council in 99 per cent of cases.

Postscript on education

'Overall,' states a report from the National Children's Bureau, 'the children from one-parent families had lower reading and arithmetic scores than the children from two-parent families.' The children concerned were at primary level, and it is easy to accept the excuse of poor housing, lack of money and exhaustion of the mother as being conducive to poor attainment. We must not, though, suppose that all one-parented children will necessarily be 'slow', just as all two-parented children cannot automatically qualify for the Brain of Britain. There is a vast overlap of grey from which, pretty regularly, a one-parent child will zip to fame on the strength of outstanding talent. What about the Duke of Wellington, the Brontës, Puccini, Lord Nelson, J. S. Bach, Byron, Irving Berlin, Jenny Lind? You could count one-parent super-folk instead of sheep ad infinitum.

Personally I am a great believer in teaching a child to read before he starts school at five. Some are ready to recognize words at three years old, so don't hold them back. All mine began on the Ladybird Key Reading Scheme: as little as ten minutes a day at first, building up to great slabs of eager time until fluency quietly took over. The infants' class is then a piece of cake. But don't push a child who isn't ready.

Another worthwhile exercise is based on the judicious use of a cassette-player. My older children were little in the era before cassettes were invented, but the younger ones have been brought up to regard the player as the natural accompaniment to pre-sleep. I record basic general knowledge to match the age of the child concerned and, after he's tucked up in bed, the tape's played back to him. The same material is played several evenings in a row, until the information is effortlessly assimilated. Counting, the alphabet, vowels, days, months, seasons, The Lord's Prayer, tables, French verbs, special dates: all can be planned according to the receptiveness of the child. Marvellous for learning homework as well. It may sound a bit batty, I don't know: but certainly many basic facts are smoothly acquired. The child is undoubtedly 'cleverer' for it, and no matter how inert mother may be after a hard day's work the bedtime cassette looks after itself. (I do soften it up sometimes with fairy tales tucked in among the gems of infant scholarship.)

Never pour cold water on a child's exuberance: you don't know what you may be destroying. Scotch the image of the under-attaining single-parent, and swear that *your* child will have every opportunity to learn. Never mind the blind of your own tiredness: help him.

Further reading

Public Schools Year Book (Boys)
Public Schools Year Book (Girls)
Directory of Grant-Making Trusts
all at the Public Library, reference section.

See Appendix

Buttle Trust
Child Guidance Clinics
Church of England Children's Society
Cruse
Dr Barnardo's
Family First
Gingerbread
National Childminding Association
National Children's Home
National Council for One Parent Families
National Pre-School Playgroups Association
National Society for Mentally Handicapped Children
Parents National Educational Union
Salvation Army
Save the Children Fund
Social Responsibility Council
Thomas Coram Foundation

8 The one-parented child: Is he different ?

The children of a single parent must obviously find themselves in situations peculiar to their family status. This is inevitable, for one cannot go about swearing that one is two. But situations need not spawn problems, and few enough real problems are exclusively peculiar to the Linear Exception. Attendant upon, perhaps, but not inseparable from.

How often, though, are our children more-or-less presumed to breed complications? Delinquency and the broken home syndrome: truancy and the latch-key child; adolescent rebellion against the single parent; emotional messes stemming from deprivation of paternal (maternal) proximity: each one could constitute a sub-heading on its own. And all we can feebly do is to swallow hard and admit that some one-parented children present troubles which need precise handling – sometimes by experts. Then balance that against two-parented children in a similar muddle. The single-parent family seldom of itself causes problems.

A psychologist, for instance (whom I later discovered was at the time living away from his wife and sons), once rounded on me for bringing up my family – in particular my boys – without professional counselling. It was presupposed that these adolescents would be emotionally haywire without a father in the home. My assurance that the boys were not entirely bereft of male company and that a large proportion of their teachers were men was superciliously waved aside as unfairly levering parental responsibility on to overworked school-teachers. In the face of such crushing opinions the single parent can but sweat, stammer and go to ground.

It's true that certain shortcomings create certain minor crises, but that doesn't imply that we ought constantly to pluck at the psychologist's elbow. As the sole adult decision-maker we generally should be able to sort matters out for ourselves, recognizing the problems for what they are, drawing such children back into the warmth of security through our own understanding and loving care. Concentrate on that rather than bolt to a counsellor at the first uneasy whimper.

All disturbed children – and admit that many one-parented children *are* disturbed at the start of the new family lifestyle – display certain symptoms. Indeed, the several children within a single family may express their sense of shock each in different ways: just as a two-parent child will react adversely to such as hospitalization, change of school, the arrival of an infant sibling.

We may be confronted (more or less in order of chance) with:

attention-seeking, sometimes called 'showing off' or 'bad manners' (all ages);
lying and/or stealing (all ages, but mainly older and teenage);
bedwetting (rarely after teenage);
nailbiting or other 'nervous' habits (rarely after teenage);
school phobia (unusual, but between nine and fourteen if at all);
running away – or running back (frequently planned by any child above six or seven years old but seldom carried out).

The most impressionable ages, in connection with breaking up, would seem to be around the years eight to fourteen. Younger children are more resilient, more trusting, less curious as to events leading up to the collapse. Older teenagers are capable of acting as judges within themselves and often they are enormously comforting to the remaining parent, for they are able to comprehend the current emotional upheaval as a subject on its own, not solely in relation to their own demands.

One-parent children are usually far and away more independent than most of their contemporaries. The four-year-old can make the tea. At nine he can prepare, cook and serve supper. He has his responsibility for certain jobs because, one down, all hands must be utilized.

Sometimes the eldest would seem to assume proxy parenthood almost as a matter of course. Might this be a natural gravitation, at one remove? Or a desire to simulate the Triangular norm? Those who study social phenomena would probably back the latter theory; the child's hidden yearning to appear the same as his peers.

John, at nineteen, has been the man in our house for years. I don't actually press responsibilities upon him, yet it never occurs to me that he'll do otherwise than organize the garden and the animals, put up the fences, saw the logs. One does not have to ask him, nor does this labour appear to be wrung from him by way of bounden duty.

'I wouldn't be up to much if I didn't,' is the modest explanation he gives of his undoubted role as male head of this tribe. Having grown up with babies and children he is himself an excellent surrogate parent, attentive to the demands of small voices.

'John, let me come to the village with you, oh, please?'

He also dispenses punitive treatment and spontaneous generosity in just the correct proportions.

'Why isn't there any kindling, David? Have you given up your job or something? I only hope you're not expecting any pocket-money at the end of the week?'

David is ten. His job, for which John pays him, is to supply a daily quota of fire-lighting sticks. If the work isn't done – even if it's done poorly or in bad grace – John is quite capable of carrying out his threat. No pocket-money.

Another day, when the little adopted boys acted strictly up to scratch, he may return from the shops with a football with no birthday in sight. Just a reward affectionately given. Do these boys at the lower end of the family, adopted from single mothers by a single mother, really miss out by not having a bona fide father? Sometimes I can easily persuade myself that they actually gain, because the cohesion within this family is so enormously strengthened by its teenagers. Not only John, who is serious about his headship, but by Jasmine with her quiet tidying up, by Jackie's bossiness over manners and her magic production of Lapsang Souchong or Sainsbury's sherry at times of low blood count, by useless Sebastian's laughter and love of life, by Helen's maternal instinct and prowess in the kitchen. All, in their separate ways, are uncommonly mature: not with weight of obvious cares (though all have had their cares, some deeper than others) but rather with a very special sense of buoyancy.

I suspect, then, that many one-parented teenagers feel a deep commitment towards family, and this may be more easily expressed in deeds than in words. The emotion may even be masked by gauche behaviour: occasionally all outward signs of belonging seem to be flung out of the window. Under whatever conditions it's up to us to let them know that we do appreciate their worth, to let them know that we couldn't do without them. (I qualify that last statement: don't push your dependence so far that they feel tied to you for ever, guilty for wanting to go out into the world. That's bad.)

Missing identity The child who has been fatherless since babyhood misses out on knowing, fully, his own self. Widowed mothers will find it easy to talk to him of father: there will be photographs in the house. He will know what father's job was, may even learn what father was like when he was a little boy. The picture may be presented again by paternal grandparents.

The young child of divorce may grow up with a blank where his father-image ought to be. He may not let on that he is aware of this blank: perhaps he is conscious that this is a taboo subject. Yet he has a right to know the other half of his biology, even if he can never know the man in person. Somehow we must bring ourselves to build up, gradually, a mental picture for the child. No need to exhibit our adult opinions of the man's behaviour, friends or habits; just a clear impression of what he looked like, how tall he was, fat or thin, bald or bearded; little points which help to make a picture real. A photograph is best of all.

Divided loyalties Sebastian points out that it's a bore as well as being embarrassing and on occasion confusing when, while staying with father, he is surreptitiously reminded of my faults, while at home, with me, he's sometimes treated to a similar monologue about father. This behaviour of ours is indefensible, more especially after so long apart. All I can do is admit my shame and try like mad to slot that type of grumbling away under bigger and better thoughts in a Positive line. It goes to illustrate, though, how easy it is to slip up and let out the once-boiling bitterness in spite of knowing it must be hidden at all costs. Parents who are other than divorced or separated won't have this trap waiting for them: be grateful. It's more difficult to circumnavigate than you'd imagine possible. Resolve anew, and be comforted after lapses that we all let rip sometimes.

Rejection of the absent parent This would seem to apply to boys more than girls. The awful thing is that our baser selves are relieved (even flattered) when the ritual of regular visiting modifies, often falls off altogether.

'I'm glad the bitch is gone!' says one six-year-old boy vehemently – a child of generally inoffensive vocabulary – after seeing his mother.

His sister, who presumably encountered the same qualities in her mother as did the boy, gladly goes off for school-holiday weeks with her. The father, a man of infinite fairness who, at the time of separation, agreed to generous access on the most friendly terms, is being worn to a rag. He feels his son's opinion has a right to be considered, that the boy ought not to be forced to go out with his mother, yet he shrinks from appearing the villain of the piece, the catalyst who has redirected the boy's affection. At present the child simply takes off. When he knows his mother is calling he is with friends in some distant corner of the housing estate. This father accepts one incident at a time, letting the girl go, excusing her brother. In such a position it would be best to ask help of a social worker or probation officer, a go-between, who could put the boy's case quietly to the mother and work out a new contact system with her. It is often impossible for estranged parents to thrash this sort of thing out for themselves without overt bitterness.

Older boys or girls may be no more rational than the younger ones in spite of being able to explain their attitudes more freely. One eleven-year-old developed a real fear of his father, cried and ran from the room when this man drove up to collect him. The mother recognized the same symptoms of terror as she herself experienced when coming face-to-face with her ex-husband: profuse sweating, shaking body, inability to speak. Luckily on this occasion there was a mutual friend present, so that although at first the father insisted that the boy be made to go on holiday, in fact he was ultimately persuaded to leave the child behind.

It seems likely that this boy, though ostensibly protected from the grosser aspects of his warring parents separation, had observed his mother's emotions intelligently and was frightened for her. He was going to leave her alone. Could he, indeed, be sure that she would still be at home when he returned? Which brings us neatly to:

School phobia This is the most devastating experience. It has nothing whatever to do with 'truanting'. Phobia is fear, even a deadly terror, when a child would put up with anything rather than go to school – that institution of mental torture. This poisonous antipathy to school is one that strikes the Linear child occasionally, and with understandable reason. Indeed, we have once in our own family experienced this crisis. It's a phase I hope never to encounter again. It inspires bewilderment and helplessness in the parent and despair of an almost suicidal order in the child. The cooperation of peripheral education workers is essential if the child is not going to be driven into broken submission or total withdrawal.

The trigger behind school phobia is, very often, a terror of losing the remaining parent. Having left, for instance, father in the family home; having removed to a new environment and new school; eliciting, perhaps, that to talk about Daddy is unwelcome; being perplexed about the role Mother now plays as 'head of the family', his world has been pulled apart and he is at a loss to understand on the emotional level what it is all about. He may remember arguments between his parents, he may have seen his mother crying, shattered or fraught. What he does understand is that he has lost one parent: thus he is going to make absolutely certain that he doesn't lose the other one.

At home he is fine. He is usually very helpful and very good. Weekends are lovely: he can laugh, go out (not too far), help with shopping, change the library books, in fact behave as any other eleven-year-old might. (Rarely does it strike younger, less rarely older: in essence this is early adolescent affliction). On Sunday night he will refuse supper as he feels sick: he goes to bed punctually and very quietly. When you go in to say good-night he will not be reading. He will be pale, frightened-looking, dreading tomorrow. In the morning he may actually be sick, will shake uncontrollably, beg and cry not to be forced to go to school.

After the shock he's already sustained nothing can reassure him that home – this new home – is safe.

This is a picture of school phobia at its worst.

Try, impatient as you feel beneath your own anguish, to project yourself under his skin, feel how he feels. Don't send him to school. It is tantamount to rejecting him: and he has to live with that doubt and terror all day. In his present state he will learn nothing, will possibly worsen matters by drawing attention to himself – a 'big boy' upset at school.

Contact his head teacher straight away and let him know what's happening. Ask for the educational psychologist to call in – or make an appointment to see him at his clinic. This is serious enough for expert help, however independent you imagine you are. What you might well aim for is permission (if only temporarily) to teach the boy at home (see chapter 7).

One twelve-year-old had four terms of home-teaching before he gained courage enough to try school again: a new school of his own choice and, surprisingly enough, a boarding school. (The County Education Authorities paid the fees.) The first half of that first term was bad, though less bad than the old days of phobia. He was desperately home-sick, walked twenty-two miles back after the initial three days, had swollen eyes and was without appetite for six weeks. Then, rather faster than gradually, he settled down. At the end of that first term he was 'one of the boys', soccer-playing, midnight-feasting, hanging smaller boys out of the dormitory windows by their heels.

Like most setbacks school phobia seems to go on for ever. Like most setbacks you wake up one day to realize the problem fizzled out weeks ago, imperceptibly. The point to remember most is that the child needs love, needs his questions answered truthfully, needs above all to build up his trust in the present. Never, never write off his fear as 'babyish', 'stupid', 'naughty'. Work with him, gently, through it.

General knowledge Parents are divided on whether it's better for teachers to know about a child's home circumstances or to remain in ignorance. I'm in favour of teachers knowing. I think they can't really make an understanding job of teaching the child unless they are aware of his stresses and strains. The anti-telling group maintains that teachers have been geared to expect one-parented children to do less well, on average, than their Triangular contemporaries. This expectation filters through, even subconsciously, and the children are – so the anti's believe – given less individual time, less strengthening of confidence.

The point is that most children, sooner or later, will let the cat out of the bag, so why put off the day? Also, especially with smaller, newer-to-school children, comes the confusion of making, say, a Father's Day (Mother's Day) card when, in fact, there is no father (mother) to receive it. 'Ask Mum so-and-so ...' or 'Ask Dad so-and-so ...' What price the poor infant teacher? Yes, she must be told essential facts if she is to integrate the new child humanely.

Names can cause confusion. Surnames, that is. Sometimes a mother will revert to her maiden name or take on any other she fancies. Whether the children also change their surname is – if they're old enough to decide – up to them. Contrary to popular belief there is no obligation to carry your father's name, nor any obligation to give it up even if the head of the family does so. Younger children often want to take mother's new name because of recognition at school. However, if father holds joint custody he ought to be consulted (if he's a consultable sort of person) before under-sixteens do a name-change. No official deed is necessary, though it's useful for occasions when you have to prove who you are or were (on income tax and official forms, etc.). Children's names may be included in the same deed as the parent's. Any solicitor will draw this up for a tenner or thereabouts. It is not the Green Form.

Delinquency, whatever that might mean, crops up like an adolescent pimple at the mention of 'broken homes', 'separated parents' and our all-lumped-together-regardless 'problem families'. Why our marvellous children should be expected to break the law in excess of Triangular children I cannot understand. If anything, because most of us are at pains to prove that we can bring up a child single-handed, we are perhaps stricter – and I hope more generous with ourselves (we don't have another adult to 'give' to) – than father-plus-mother. The only delinquents who have found shelter under this roof have been foster children, teenagers, from two-parent backgrounds. Indeed the University of Kent, in a recent survey, found that the children of one-parent families were no more subject to delinquency than other children until the constant parent remarried. So look out.

The local Probation Officer is the man to go to if you're in need of help over a child who's becoming genuinely out of control. Or the Juvenile Liaison Officer (not just *any* old policeman) at your police station. No need to wait for real trouble: this move can be preventive. Worries about drugs should also be unburdened in the same direction for sympathetic and constructive advice. In the case of drugs queries there's no obligation to give your name, nor that of your child: in certain areas it is positively detrimental for a boy to have a label attached at police level.

Supposing a teenager – or younger – is picked up by the police? What rights has the parent then? If over sixteen the boy or girl is treated as an adult. You will in all likelihood be informed of the child's whereabouts and the charge (if any) made against him. You may ask to see him immediately (but must abide by official consent or refusal) and may alert a solicitor. If sixteen or under the police must let you know at once if they hold your child. If you're not on the telephone they will get a police car to the house and you are at liberty to return to the police station straight away. If this is a first, and minor, offence there is every likelihood of the boy or girl being let off with a caution and allowed home. If the trouble is more severe the Social Services Department may become involved and the child could, for the time being, be removed to a Community Home or a more secure council-run establishment. Lose no time in contacting a solicitor for proper advice. The CAB will suggest the best firm to approach if you are at a loss to choose for yourself.

Bedwetting, politely referred to as nocturnal enuresis, which I always think sounds like some sort of twilight mammal, can strike the new single-parent like the plague. Why a child's bladder should act as a barometer to his emotional state, heaven knows: but it does. Children (boys in particular) who have been dry for months, years even, begin to sleep afloat. This has nothing at all to do with filling up on squash at supper time or drinking the tooth-mug water. Indeed, the child may have taken no liquid for hours before bedtime, but will still be awash by morning. 'Ten o'clock potting' doesn't do much good either. One of the extraordinary things about bedwetting is that frequency is often speeded up. In bed by eight, wet by nine, wet again at eleven, again by, say two and on till the sodden awakening. The washing, particularly through a British autumn or winter, can send one berserk.

People professional and lay will fall over themselves to tell you to 'leave things', that the phase will stop of its own accord, to build up the child's confidence and, above all, to 'look for the root cause' (as if one didn't know!). People professional and lay might be interested to learn that bedwetting often doesn't stop of its own accord, even in children who have been dry before the overwhelming upset.

The social offshoots of bedwetting are grossly limiting for any child. No Cub camp, no overnight stops with schoolfriends, no holidays with relatives without the indignity of much waterproof luggage. The morning smell of the bedwetter and his room – let's not be delicate about that either. The sufferer, in short, isn't indifferent (as many will suggest he is) to the situation. He doesn't enjoy being the artist of such wringing havoc and we don't like the daily washing of sheets and pyjamas. (Nappies, suggests someone, are all right for two/three/four-year-olds, but hugely *infra dig* for older children, inadequate by area too, and almost totally frustrating for the boy who does wake in the night and tries to get to the potty in time.)

The answer lies in that miracle of simple invention, The Buzzer. I've twice resorted to hiring The Buzzer, once for a ten-year-old who dried out at the usual age of about two-and-a-half, then started off again at about five and never dried out by his own effort again. Once for a six-year-old who had never been dry at night and often woke in such a record-breaking pool that he was dripping (no lies) from hair to feet. In both instances the children were dry – and have ever-after been dry – within a fortnight. Transformed characters, too, with their new freedom and without any more of the additional or transferred emotional problems forecast by the 'don't worry them' brigade.

The Buzzer serves the function of alerting the mind to the inclinations of the bladder. The child sleeps over two draw-sheets between which tinfoil pads are inserted. These foil pads are wired up to a simple battery-fired bell (there is *no* possibility of electric shock). The top pad is perforated, so urine seeps through causing a short circuit which sets off an ear-splitting buzz. The child gets out of bed, finishes performing in the potty, changes his own drawsheets, and gets off to sleep again.

After a few nights he wakes before he begins to wet himself: mind and bladder are in touch! (Just out of interest the ancient Chinese used a similar system, though the buzzer was replaced by a species of toad in a muslin bag, strapped to the child's loins. This toad croaked loudly with indignation when wetted.)

Buzzers may be hired direct from various agencies, or obtained for free through family doctors or clinics. Beware, though, some clinics are anti-buzzer and will tell you to persevere, praise the child for the occasional dry night (if any) and never, never show your impatience. In that case hire The Buzzer independently.

I'm sorry to have gone on about bedwetting so much, but, of all behaviour setbacks presented to me, bedwetting has been the most often mentioned. Clearly it bothers a lot of single parents who already have masses of extra work to do and plenty of two-parents as well no doubt. Simply reading the grateful letters from satisfied clients, sent along in the parcel when you hire The Buzzer, can make your hair stand on end, for instance elderly gentlemen who had never had a dry night, been denied marriage, holidays, almost turned recluse, until freed from bondage by the latter-day toad. It makes you wonder. Let us, anyway, extricate our children from the rising waters.

Daytime incontinence after an emotional upheaval isn't all that unusual, but it can take the new one-parent child unawares. It is generally a lapse of short duration, triggered off, literally, by nervousness and insecurity. The more you rant and rage the longer the phase is likely to last. Indeed, the very act of ranting can cause the poor child to pee uncontrollable floods on the spot. Try to keep calm, don't fuss. Just change the pants and let him or her know you care.

Opposite to the children who turn against the absent parent are those who blame the parent with whom they are living for depriving them of normal family life. This can be actual or implied. Partly the children feel sorry for the father (mother) left behind: 'Daddy will be so lonely. Who'll do his ironing? Do you think he'll be able to manage the blender?' Sometimes the seeming callousness of the active one-parent is reflected in the daughter's solicitous care for the absent and inactive one. She takes on the guilt which she feels her mother ought to display. She elects to go to him for Christmas, birthday, Easter – times when her sweet nature is repelled by the thought of him being alone. She must be allowed to go, however much it hurts, not for the reasons she imagines, but for her own peace of mind.

She is the reverse, if you like, of the six-year-old who refuses to go to his mother for holidays.

Nailbiting can start in previously non-nibbling children after family upheaval. It's harder than anything to stop because the habit really is unconsciously done. Some parents don't mind the merry little click-click as their children snap away while reading, watching TV, settling down to sleep. Others do. Nasty stuff painted on the fingers is the only outwardly imposed cure that seems to work – and then it's not always certain. There are various proprietary brands of cure on the market. The best still seems to be the old-fashioned bitter aloes, which some chemists are reluctant to sell you. It comes in liquid or crystals (the crystals you dissolve). The drawback is that aloe has a mildly aperient effect, so children who go on biting regardless of the gallish taste can get diarrhoea. Proceed cautiously.

Unless the habit really sets your teeth on edge then it's probably better to leave things as they are until the child wants to stop – usually at puberty for girls, might be never for boys. The bind is that the habit often persists long after the upset promoting its inception has long blown over.

Nightmares, restlessness and sleep-talking are sure signs of a worried or disturbed child. We all know that our own problems tend to come back in sleep (or to prevent sleep): it's the same for children. Peaceful nights will come once the new lifestyle is established, for rarely do bogies disrupt the sleep of a long-term one-parenter. Go along with the child's needs: it's your presence he wants when he wakes from a bad dream. Take him into bed with you: often a few reassuring words spoken while he's still half asleep will calm him. Always see him into his own bed yourself, tuck him up, see he's comfortable, that he has a drink if he's that sort of a boy, and a potty if he's that sort of a one. Leave his door and/or curtains open should he want it that way. Leave the landing light on (never mind the bill). Above all, love the child. There's no need to go for sleep draughts, guidance clinics, Ovaltine. If you have a cassette or record player use it as sleep-inducer. I've found Debussy and Vivaldi good sedatives, but don't go out to buy anything specially. The point is to play the soporifics very softly and in a poor light.

The cuckoo symptom Children once settled within the one-parent way of life may genuinely dread mother (father) re-marrying. The older they grow the more the resentment of any intrusion by even remotely prospective step-parents. My teen-agers have, without exception, been rude and awful to any man with the hint of a spark in his eye. I don't altogether blame them: in their vulnerable position I would probably feel the same. Having made a bloomer of one marriage I can see no reason why they should trust me to do better with a second. Peace reigns in our house and the last thing we want is a new man dictating the colour of the emulsion or how he likes his eggs boiled. When they are knowing, school-aged, mother-guarding people, what then? Older children often do actually mind. They are great moralists and great observers too: 'Oh, how could you, Mummy,' they accuse ... 'he's got hairs up his nose.'

Younger children, sub-teens, don't seem to suffer this step-parent dread. A little bit of the opposite: they tend to play to the audience, wheedle for attention, work on his ego, he is there to be entertained by them, not as a threat to their way of life.

Attention-seeking explains itself. It's a relatively new term stemming from the old idea of 'being naughty'. It indicates, in every case without exception, that the child needs more loving. Attention-seeking happens quite often after one parent has left, and more so if there's a change of house and school as well. Getting noticed by being bad is almost as satisfactory to the child as getting noticed by being good. (Goodness is often taken for granted and goes unpraised, badness raises the parental blood-pressure and is guaranteed to work.) The solution is to love the child, however ghastly and hungry-for-affection he may be. Let him help with the chores, with cooking, take him with you when you go out, never send him upstairs alone to bed, go and tuck him in, read that story, sing the inane rhymes he likes. Get it through to him, fast, that he is your best thing in the world, and that he is safe with you.

The older attention-seeking child will steal from shops or

from you, tell lies, break things on purpose, hide objects that he knows you'll want – purse, glasses, coffee, Child Benefit Book – and then reap the praise when, after having watched you frenziedly hunt from attic to cellar, he miraculously 'finds' it in a place you've checked a dozen times. The same loving, on an upgraded level, goes for his problem: but one must be firm as iron over the shop-stealing. Go with the child to the store, see he returns the stolen goods (usually sweets) or at least pays for them and apologizes to the shopkeeper. It is such a shaming experience that he'll probably never steal again.

Babies Daughters of single mothers stand more chance, statistically, of producing a baby out of marriage than do girls from a two-parent home. Even if that two-parent home lasted a limited time only. The primary reason for most accidental conceptions out of marriage is, ironically, a hunger for (not a surfeit of) love. The unloved snatch at whatever affection is offered. The coming of a baby, in turn, provides the girl with an object upon which to bestow love. It should be a self-solving problem but somehow it never is. If we feel strongly about random babies then we must be careful beyond doubt that our own daughters know they are wanted, loved, understood. Our sons too. Promote contraception for teenagers and don't give the impression that any subject is taboo. As soon as my daughters reach puberty, before sometimes, I make certain that they undertand all babies are welcome in our family. Never be censorious, or appear to be. Never (this is my hang-up, it needn't be yours) aid and abet an abortion ... it's your grandchild. Personally I find the mother/daughter tie very binding within the Linear Family. Binding, not possessive.

So many of the difficulties which our one-parented children encounter seem to have mirror-images. The child goes along with us or kicks against us: he reverts to babyishness or shoulders the premature burden of adult responsibility: he fears we may reject him or he seeks to reject us. However, the odds are that he will present no over-sensitivity other than the most transient. We need not harp back to the guilt-trap of 'Should I have stayed for the sake of the children?' That question was let loose in the world only to make us turn tail into a false morality. If the partnership was so awful that we are better out of it, then they are better out of it too. Not to mention the absent parent.

See Appendix

Child Guidance Clinics
CAB
Cruse
Family Care
Gingerbread Advice
Mothers' Union
Parent Lifeline
National Federation of Solo Clubs
Salvation Army

9 The emotional hazards of being a child-tied one-parent

A heavy degree of isolation is inherent in the very nature of the half-family. Whether, given time, we thrash about in order to rejoin the rest of the world, or spin a soft web around ourselves and burrow inwards, depends largely upon our basic natures. Gregarious or solitary? In which direction do we, as individuals, swing?

At the beginning of being alone with the children, making a living and keeping house, battling with legalities and recovering from shock, there is little time for socializing with other people. The primal urge to survive obliterates all but essential outside contact. We have probably never done so much in our lives so all we ask of any spare time is the opportunity to sleep. This goes for numbers of us. The most dangerous pitfall during this early period of mental and physical exhaustion is that of emotionally neglecting the children – at a time when they desperately need reassurance of our love and sanity. We tend to be so involved in our own struggle that we fail to allow for the odd hours when simply 'being normal' with the children is the number-one Must. It's useless, of course, trying to con them into thinking that life is progressing as it always has done: it will never be the same for them, exactly. The least we can do, though, is ensure that the changeover sticks as closely to their usual routine as practicable. Don't refuse to join in that never-ending game of Monopoly. Don't say 'Yes, darling, but could you possibly tell me about it later?' Pinch great chunks out of your day to give to them.

The passage of time and the boredom of repetition – not to mention the baby's progress towards reason – enables us to see out a little. The need for other humans creeps back. Particularly at night. One misses a man in the bed (though a child is warm in winter). This gap between one day and the next can be almost unbearably arid and it may help, in avoidance of self-pity, to offer up a prayer of gratitude that we, unlike so many other 'adults alone', have children to love and to love us.

Something to make the present worth working for: otherwise why opt for this abbreviated lifestyle?

As much as anything we probably miss real conversation, real talk. Male conversation particularly. Children's talk is often enchanting, and as they grow older it is stimulating and fun, even baby talk isn't all that bad in spite of how it sounds off-stage: but these can't ever be the same as one adult level with another. A lot of one-parents talk to themselves – sing, recite poetry, exercise aloud their powers of mental arithmetic – just like others who choose to live alone. I find talking to myself helps with the more routine chores: sometimes it's a fill-in for the radio when the programme isn't up to much. The radio is a great boon and I suffer withdrawal symptoms when the batteries run out on shop-closing day. It is my constant educator: the habits of the common shrew; the working parts of a trade union; the private and tragic private life of Isabella Beeton – the captive mind is ever widened, ever 'improved'.

However, look out when you move on to the television. Constant telly-watching, some psychologist says, is a symptom of depression (symptom, or result of?). Everyone knows you can't do much while watching, whereas radio oozes quietly out while you wash, scrub, type, or cook. The telly is more of a drug as well: an effortless escape into a substitute world. I've met people who say 'good evening' to quizmasters and 'thank you' to the man who reads the news. Take stock when you find yourself smiling a welcome and don't fall into the old pit of imagining the telly is a cure for loneliness. It only hides it. Real people are better and they're around if you care to make an effort. I'm not saying don't have a telly: by all means, do. But don't lean upon it emotionally.

It may be tranquillizing to the newly independent to know that all one-parents, however 'capable' or 'happy', experience the odd bout of rock-bottom loneliness, and the odder, tougher drag of grey and spiritless inertia too. It is inevitable. Dreams of rescue and giddy new love tend to alternate with fears of an unshared old age. Barely understood worries dodge from side to side in the head. We ache for someone else to help with the double quota of work; make just some of the decisions; get up to feed the crying child at 2 a.m. If we didn't occasionally feel like this we'd probably be too boringly saintly to bear. Accept these troughs of low as an integral part of The Linear life and if you have any secret formulae to stem the tide of isolation, then use them: chocolate; alcohol; fags; a good howl; wild bouts of noisy housework or furniture moving; writing an agonizingly subjective poem; or even deliberate overwork; something that might distract you from troubles, and rage. I've applied all these with good effect. Work at being alone, and by that I mean alone as an adult. Solitude more than anything makes one realize one's own potential, answers the question – 'Who am I?'

Overeating is a lurking hazard. One of my friends weighs nineteen stone. Most of us are overweight, if only marginally.

The diet of the poor is unerringly stoutening. We tend to eat at the same time as the children: beans on toast and macaroni cheese: and what makes them grow makes us grow too. Carbohydrates are relatively cheap. Proteins and fruit are expensive. It's as simple as that.

Anxiety, boredom, shock, mental emptiness, can all stimulate a lurch towards the bread-bin. The electricity bill may be tempered by a jam sandwich; the unearthly gap through which we struggle while the children are visiting father is made more tolerable by a packet of plain biscuits.

The fact that our children are just about the only people who actually see us naked renders any change less urgent (one good reason for having a lover). Certainly a detached look at ourselves in a long glass is aesthetically necessary. The old Life Assurance test is a useful guide: if you can pick up a handful of surplus at the side of the ribs – you're too fat.

Will-power, strengthened by a new positivism, is the only way out. On our stingy budget we cannot eat differently, so we must eat less. A child's innocent remark helps. One little girl became mysteriously unwell so that she couldn't go to school on Sports Day. Later she confided in an older sister that she'd 'put it on' so that her mother wouldn't go. 'I couldn't face her being seen,' the child said. And mother overheard. Within three months she'd lost a couple of stone.

Depression dive-bombs at us periodically – literally periodically. And for the lone mother there is no ease-up during the off-days of pre-menstrual tension. In truth, seldom does the universe become so black that we creep to the doctor for tranquillizers: often, on the other hand, we must resort to our own pet quackery, from aspirin upwards. Always bear in mind that PMT is what it is, and it is brief. Remember, too, that children react like litmus to our own moods. When we are more likely to show impatience, intolerance, lack of understanding, we should be on guard.

Depression of a more fundamental nature is more difficult to lose. It can build up from a multitude of minor causes; from inadequacies, guilt, financial strain, the awful behaviour of children. It is perhaps the first outward sign of a fear of failure, the top side of a slide into hopelessness. And when we fail, even on one single point, we load the vulnerability of our children. Crisis may only be an inch away. Action, even in our state of lethargy, becomes imperative.

Only the iron-willed can respond to 'pull your socks up' at so late a stage: who cares, after all, whether those socks sag dismally around the ankles? Try, though, to get as far as isolating the main worries. Do this while the children are at school, or in bed, when you know you have a quiet hour absolutely to yourself, and regard this hour as Step One out of the awful chasm. If you pinpoint say, lack of money as the chief burden, resolve to ask for help at the appropriate door tomorrow. (See addresses of relevant help organizations in Appendix.) Don't procrastinate. Write it down. In your state you're quite capable of forgetting today's thoughts by tomorrow morning. Deal with this problem first, then tackle the next. Depression can create a sort of mental indigestion and calls for very gentle sorting out: if you rush at it all at once you're back where you started. Know that, if you want to remain a balanced one-parent family, then the threatening depression must be overcome, otherwise what chance is there of a happy time for your children? Not to mention the fifty years which may still remain of your own lifespan? Apply to a doctor, obviously, if you can't make it a DIY job. But for heaven's sake be careful where you keep those lethal tranquillizing pills.

Rejection and guilt are interrelated. Both are emotions of a chance nature, unlike loneliness and depression which hit us all at some point – whether we choose to admit it or not. Women whose men have left them, rather than vice versa, suffer rejection blues. One mother says, 'The feeling of being unloved and unlovely comes in great gusts,' yet few of us are so unremittingly hideous that we're powerless to save our faces or figures, or minds, come to that. Rejection could be equated with a period of mourning, an elemental transition from the two-sided to the one-sided life. Like the bereaved, the rejected tend to shut themselves away: they neither seek nor want outside stimulus. I believe this is an essential quiet time in which to repair and recover and to meet our children in their new roles too.

Many families, in the early days of one-parenting, must concentrate exclusively upon their future structure in order to recognize their day-to-day strengths and weaknesses. There must be eventual emergence from this self-imposed purdah; for the family turned in upon itself *in perpetuam* tightens into a ball of neuroses. The rejected mother feels herself to be accepted only by her children – small beings both too young and too physically attached to form any discriminative analysis of her qualities. The beginning of the way out may lie in some initial act as simple as buying a pot of cold cream, as easy as refurbishing the face. A participating world outside her own narrow confines must be met: a world of people, many with problems which she herself may be able to lighten through her own experiences. Parent-teacher evenings at the children's school, local Gingerbread, even the Welfare Clinic, all present introductory opportunities to form contact. As with many outward-going movements, self-respect – the other side of rejection – will come in.

A widow with sons of eleven and eight, alone for two years, writes 'I am not at all unhappy now and in fact would not change my life-style very readily. One of the incredible aspects of other people's attitudes is the assumption that one is the poor relation and miserable with it. Whereas, in fact, once the anguish of loss was over, it would have been positively self-indulgent continuously to look back and grieve all the time. Sometimes I look at all those supposedly lucky and fulfilled people who think I have lost out and marvel at their blinkered approach to life. I am sure I was like them once, but having survival forced upon one certainly clears the mind wonderfully of all the bunkum attached to "middle-class" life. Incidentally, I don't think "working-class" people suffer this isolation quite so much. I would have a bet that the middle-class one-parent families suffer more from rejection than others do.'

Guilt may be geared towards the man (What did I do wrong? What could I have done to save us?) or towards the situation in which the children find themselves now (Will they suffer? Will they blame me?). Unlike the rejected parent, the guilt-ridden parent needs to talk. She wants her questions answered. She wants to be told it's not really her fault. And often she is a gross bore, because the questions have no precise form, no precise answer. If guilt happens to be your own hang-up, watch out, and take comfort from the knowledge that it, like bitterness, often wears off in time. The tragedy is that it causes havoc along the way to extinction. Your constant harping makes people run a mile and can lose you good friends. Recognize it for the destroyer it is before it lands you in a mess, and if the going's too hard don't think it's too trifling for professional advice. Go to somebody whose job it is to listen and put you out of your misery. This needn't cost you anything. Your doctor or Health Visitor could get you an appointment to see a psychologist on the National Health. The Marriage Guidance Council may be approached direct: they are very used to helping single-parent families, so the fact that you are no longer married is neither here nor there to them. Private-practice psychologists are expensive and are to be avoided by single-parents: though some independent ones hold Talk-Ins, where groups of 'patients' can discuss their feelings until those problems die of exhaustion. *Families Need Fathers* is organized by one such public-spirited psychologist and meetings are regularly held in London. There is no charge for participation, and it's open to mothers as well as fathers.

It's probably not necessary to remind you that cash compensation for emotional problems is counter-productive.

Boredom seems to afflict lone fathers more than lone mothers. The chores as always are endless and, curiously, men seem more fastidious than women. Women don't as often carry a conscience when housework falls behind. I think fathers are, possibly, trying to show how efficiently they can manage without a woman. One father certainly told me that although he loathed ironing he was very particular about his children's clothes: his wife, he explained, had always made a point of turning them out neatly. Was his stint at the ironing-board a hang-over from his married days, or a sensible decision that every domestic detail should go on as before for the children's sake?

Simply speeding things up often helps to prevent boredom. Give yourself a time limit for the sitting-room or the mending and after that leave it. Go out, do something you enjoy. Read, talk, eat an apple, lose yourself. Try to dismiss your sense of what should and what shouldn't be accomplished in order to conform. Does it really matter if there's dust under the bed?

'I turn up the hi-fi as high as it'll go and simply blast the boredom out,' says one father-alone. Worth a try, but make sure of the neighbours first.

List-making is another way of getting through the essentials of the day without sinking into boredom. Vary the type of chore hour by hour and don't let two days run to the same pattern. One single mother I know, tied at home with three children under school age and also running a bed-and-breakfast service through the summer, works a system whereby she does two 'essential' jobs before she allows herself a 'nice' one. It's all a game really, but it does help to lift the fog of domestic repetition.

The point to remember about boredom is that it can always be counteracted to a large extent by mental effort. If we're bored then ten-to-one we're boring. That knowledge alone is enough to spur us into action.

A single father has the outlet of pubs and clubs. Women, of course, have the right to do the same but, equality or no, few have the courage to walk into a strange pub alone.

Bitterness is a terrible thing for bursting out, even when we're trying like hell to pretend it doesn't feature. Many a woman feels her own life child-tied, turned-in after divorce, yet cannot help seeing her husband's life as new and 'free'. I'm ashamed to record that I still feel stung, ten years after, when the children return from a weekend with father. He, whose income topples ours by thousands, can afford to give them bacon for breakfast (after the cornflakes, before the toast, concurrent with the egg, mushroom, frankfurter); Coca cola by the jeroboam; fruit-and-nut by the giant slab; colour telly downstairs, black-and-white up; cups and plates all matching and a kitchen stove that does just about everything but fly. How bitchy it must sound to the lucky ones who got through the divorcing process without harsh words or fights for children. It is bitchy; I know it, and all others in this same boat know it, but, believe me, it's almost more than the soul can bear when a child comes back laden with money and goodies, throws herself into your arms and says, 'We had a marvellous time! Daddy took us to this grown-up restaurant and we had prawns and steak and pudding made from cream and wine. Then we went to the Planetarium by taxi, and Madame Tussaud's, and finished up having tea at the zoo!' But take a happy interest one must: the great sin is to show how dog-in-the-manger you feel.

Think. You wanted the children, didn't you? You like providing the wherewithal for their plain fare; you love their company and their openness? You got it.

If you mumble unresponsively to those returning children and shut your ears to their father-praising their openness will be gone, their spontaneity guarded. Nothing you say or do will change their opinion of the absent parent, yet, if you let your own feelings out too vehemently those children may learn to hide their honesty simply to string you along, even to be kind. Remember, it's not the child's fault that you separated, or never married. So count ten before you answer, and if you secretly begin to see red then start to look about for something to do to involve yourself externally: start on the washing-up, polish something, iron something, cut your nails. Reason within your head, see that your bitterness is stupid, out of place, against the children's interests. Appreciate the marvellous fact that you have them 'all the time', while he has them for only two or three short weekends a year.

Bitterness in relation to one's predicament is, if anything, more damaging than anything because it is protracted, perhaps indeed ever-present. To feel resentful about being a one-parent represents an acute form of back-pedalling, a clear case for sitting down to think about yourself absolutely objectively. What sort of a mother are you if the tenor of family life is shot through with your acid attitudes? Where on earth do you think you're taking everybody? If you truly can't bear the prospect of a manless state stretching light-years ahead, then admit it to yourself and take the first bold steps towards Relationship Two (chapter 16 for ideas). Otherwise start on One-Parent Positivism. Keep a list of daily plusses and minusses if it helps. But somehow get going on the ascent into the wholesome half-family.

A sense of *inadequacy* can be triggered off by something as commonplace as physical tiredness. 'I can't cope!' is a cry for help. It may seem hard to fit in, but honestly the most effective self-treatment for this neutral collapse is sleep. Twelve hours at least, at a stretch. Unless there's a really young baby in the house this ought to be quite easily managed. Leave all the evening chores, regardless, and go to bed as soon as the children are tucked up. Don't read, worry, answer telephone or door bell; draw the curtains, relax, and go to sleep. In the morning, who knows, the energy and will to manage may have returned. Nevertheless, do the minimum; cut daily chores down to thrice-weekly chores (hoovering, washing, ironing, shopping). Avoid long-drawn-out cooking sessions by bowing for once to instant and raw foods. Blow some money on disposable nappies. Buy time and spend it on yourself. Eat luxuries. Stop aiming at perfection and, whenever remotely possible, take to the horizontal. Try this lazy regime for as little as a single week, then look at yourself again.

If what you see is just as hopeless after this self-imposed break, then maybe you ought to try for some outside help: your local Gingerbread for preference. There you will doubtless meet someone else who has experienced the same low and emerged again. Explain your predicament to the secretary of the group and leave the introductions to her. Professional services often tend to be 'too busy' for such peripheral weaknesses.

Shyness sounds fey and juvenile. It's neither, and can be a curse for the single-parent who's been out of wider circulation for ages. It's all very well to be told 'go out and meet people', quite a different thing to be able to start making contact from scratch. The classic cure for shyness is to train yourself to concentrate totally upon the person you're talking to (or, more likely, who's talking to you). Pretend that she is the shy one and set about putting her at ease. It's yet another sort of game, and personally I find it only works to a limited degree. One's never quite oblivious of the urge to make for home.

The double-awful thing about shyness is that, very often, it manifests itself as stand-offishness. Up goes the haughty chin and the message 'unapproachable' is sent out by invisible current. Some of the most harrowing, yet compulsory, occasions of my year revolve round school Open Day, Parents' Day, Speech Day, Sports Day, Prize-giving and Summer Fair. To stand alone and probably dowdy among hatted two-parents can be mentally paralysing. It helps, whenever practicable, and sometimes when not, to take a younger child for moral support. Once I pretended an infant had dirtied himself in order to make an escape which had become imperative.

Shyness, alas, even makes any approach to single-parent social events more of an ordeal. Events which should present a shining opportunity to get to know others with similar meeting-points for conversation. Some parents tend to find these gatherings too hearty: 'One look put me off,' pronounced a rather retiring single father who, at heart, would very much like to enter into some degree of social life again. The sad truth is, of course, that this heartiness also covers an element of reticence.

Intolerance towards one's children is, from time to time, inevitable. Lone parents take all the knocks and there has to be a limit. Even the most loved child is sometimes rude, cheeky, unwittingly unkind – just when the parent is at her lowest ebb. I'd be prepared to bet there isn't one mother reading this who hasn't laid a hand in anger on her child: smacked him, shaken him, pushed him away from her. We ought not to, but we do, and sometimes, to save face, we tell ourselves that this is 'discipline', is being 'cruel to be kind', when really it serves to relieve our own feelings.

If we had someone else, I mean a partner, with whom to blow our tops over the behaviour of children for the moment out of favour, our pent-up irritation might never explode so fiercely. As it is, alone, we must learn to put the brakes on, and think before we slap or shout or humiliate a child.

The best thing, if the noise and awfulness soars off into the heights, is to get right away from it. Better to put the toddler, screaming like fury, alone in his cot (sides safely up) and shut the door on him, than administer an unreasoned smacking. For, when you feel strung up to snapping point, what begins as a corrective may well get out of control. Older children can be banished to bedroom, garden, almost anywhere: or you could huffily take yourself off to the kitchen to clatter the pots meaningfully. The point is to put distance between you and the seat of irritation, and to realize that you're not unique in experiencing such foul feelings.

The younger the child the greater the danger. A tiny infant has no communication apart from his insistent voice, and there will be times when that falsetto is impossible to bear: it's the pitch, not necessarily the duration, that is so mind-blowing. He's been fed, changed, winded, tucked up securely, yet the screaming, thrashing, red-faced decibel-breaking noise is unremittingly sustained. All mothers who live alone know this state of high tension: even harder to take if there are critical or nosy neighbours. Yet we single parents must promise ourselves that we will never, but never, hit that small baby. He can't run away from us, as an older child can, to the safety of another corner of the house: he cannot even defend the more vulnerable parts of his fragile body. Note the word fragile.

When you begin to doubt your ability to exercise control stop trying to placate this infant, at once. As with the toddler, tuck him up in his crib – no need to match yell for yell – and shut the door on him. Get out of the house, away from him, and walk, walk, walk ... compassless, until boiling point has been tempered by reason. Never mind, for once, the law's interpretation of 'neglect': this is one occasion when it becomes the lesser of two evils to leave a child alone in the house. Better a baby screaming blue murder until natural exhaustion takes over than his own parent physically punishing him during a phase of uncontrolled emotion. Now, calmly put the problem into someone else's hands. If possible get hold of a friend who can go back to the house with you, someone who will mind the baby for the next few hours while you either 'talk it out' or sleep. If you haven't anyone you can call on in such an emergency use one of the agencies listed in the Appendix, or any vicar or priest, whether you're one of their flock or not. Some doctors are approachable on this problem: others, alas, are not. One mother's GP, for instance, countered her confidence with the suggestion that what she really needed was an occasional baby-sitter, but that unfortunately the group practice was not a baby-sitting agency. End of consultation! At the other end of the scale is a report that a doctor – not even one with whom the mother and child were registered, sent round his wife to spend the evening with a distraught parent who had approached him out of the blue when she reached the end of her tether.

When the temptation to hurt a child is a recurring rather than a one-off situation then it's sensible to get in touch with Social Services. They can instigate fairly immediate counselling and maybe authorize such as a temporary Home Help or regular visitor so that some of the strain of caring solo is lifted. The NSPCC is also at the end of a telephone line: all is confidential and no uniformed officer turns up at the door to alert the neighbours. An enormous proportion of NSPCC work is, in fact, preventive like this.

We're all rotten, ranting, over-demanding, nigh-on-dangerous parents on occasion: it's just that this is part of our private selves which we generally disguise with a brave new face. It is no use pretending I'm exempt: indeed once I did take my own advice and walk out on my children. For half-an-hour I was gone, striding in any-old-direction, baby in pram before me.

The house was mouse-quiet when I returned. There was a note tucked in the letter-box, its message open to the world. 'I'm afrad to say are mummy has left us. Please leav 2 pts and well pay on saterdy'. All four heads lay angelically on their pillows, the exaggerated breathing of those feigning sleep clearly audible. I felt relieved that they would drift into real sleep knowing I had come back.

It might be said that I made the best I could out of a damned awful and petty job: those children have never forgotten that evening when I rejected them and walked out. Jokingly they throw it at me, all these years after: 'Mummy's getting ratty, mind she doesn't go off!' And the guilt and the shame reappears.

Still, I did avoid violence.

Bulk migration is when a one-parent goes shopping, to the dentist, to visit grandmother, anywhere. Being the only adult in the house, and being wary enough to know that it can be construed as neglect if we leave children alone, we all go together. Baby-sitters are a waste of precious money except for very special and unavoidable occasions. Public transport fares are expensive, so we walk, bicycle (dicky-seats for infants are still available through shops such as ubiquitous Halfords) or, if we're few enough, hitch-hike. I've always found motorists generous towards woman-plus-children, and lifts are easy once you muster the courage to put up your thumb for the first time.

'Paris and back with my twelve-year-old,' wrote a forty-year-old north-country mother, 'and all for the price of various cups of tea and coffee.' It can be done, but there can of course be problems.

How one longs, though, sometimes to walk the pavement without a child clutching either hand. It would be good to go to a theatre or cinema without taking all the tribe. But for the moment we must be content to wait for the day when the last child reaches school age, and this does come and with it a freedom to move at will between the hours of nine and three-thirty. Meanwhile, to take the drag out of troop-movement, use reins for toddlers, thus leaving shopping-bag arms free or, better, get hold of a big old-fashioned pram (WRVS, free : or Oxfam, about £2) to take two or three children plus groceries, library books, beer bottles and firewood picked out of the hedge on the way home. And stop minding about the impression you present.

For more extensive travel it's worth inquiring at British Rail about Economy Fares (half-price, certain days) and special concessionary children's fares. Used cunningly the railway costs no more than long-distance coaches, and of course train journeys are fun. Coach journeys are cramped, too hot, too cold, stuffy, sick-making and without that most essential of all child-needs – the lavatory.

Adolescent awfulness is no myth. No child escapes, not even the one who was formerly charming, polite, helpful, and loving. No parent, then, can hope to be let off a period in that particular snake-pit where the teenager's moodiness, apparent unreasonableness, relative despair and open loathing writhe about without check. Personally I've found this phase the most unspeakable of the whole business of one-parenting. If ever one needs the counsel of another close and caring adult, it's now. When the child rejects us, as he almost certainly will, we have nobody to explode to or seek comfort from. When we feel in our bones that a 'straight talk' might do the trick, or at least make the rebel able to look at himself without his rosy specs, there is nobody to give that 'straight talk'. And we dare not give it ourselves for fear of driving the situation to the brink where the one-parent child becomes the no-parent child.

So, what do we do when a thirteen-year-old, sophisticated

and grumpy, spits out, 'Sometimes I hate you!' Clearly it can't do much good to snap back, 'Same here!' One has to be loyal, to be constant as far as the will permits, to bat back with the same old love – that bedrock of the true family system.

'My elder daughter works extremely hard towards her future and is highly motivated,' writes a single mother, 'but she uses this as an excuse for doing nothing at home, knowing that I somehow compensate by being pleased with her excellent school work.' This is reiterated by the behaviour of the younger daughter who is 'at present going through a phase of being rude, indifferent, cheeky and uncooperative – yet at the same time she's willing to spend time visiting an old lady – and you'd never suspect she's got a soft heart.

'I think this behaviour is brought on by my own independent attitude, in that I refuse to mother her as if she were still at primary school. She's complained to me about my unmotherliness. Though I am proud of my children, I am not in the least bit possessive of them, unlike so many parents I see emotionally eating their children. In the process everybody gets even more screwed up.'

There is, so far as I know, no antidote to adolescent character-change. It hits them all, not least the ones who get by, all sugar and light, to eighteen or nineteen before the world's complexity (not to mention their own body's) gets too much for them and they celebrate the lot with an anti-social binge. The nice thing is, when we're patient enough to mark time, their inevitable return to normality. A return, moreover, apparently oblivious to the minor hell through which they've wrung their only parent. They have simply tunnelled through into adulthood. All we have to do is wait. By ourselves.

Physical frustration, sexual frustration We're bound to take on these two little burdens when we throw ourselves into one-parenting. Some women actually hide the fact that their husbands have left them. Perhaps it's a loophole, a last opportunity extended to the man: might he return? Is it necessary, after all, to accept imposed limits?

Yes, in truth, it is. Although we learn pretty fast how to tackle jobs generally considered to be the male's prerogative, we learn too what we cannot manage to do. I can clear the flue, push rods down the outside drains, cart hay, turn over quarter-of-an-acre with an ordinary spade; I can paint walls and wood-work, just about replace broken window panes, passably lay new plastic flooring. These, if you like, are the 'father's-side' of my accomplishments, new since one-parenting. On the other hand, try as I may, roof-slate-replacing and upper-window painting, once giddily attempted, must be written off as beyond my powers. I want to make the upstairs windows match the lower, but I can't. I am chicken about the ladder. We all have lists of household and domestic things we can do, lists of those we can't. The frustration over the inefficiency of our own bodies sometimes drives us to nailbiting, makes us resent the lack of male help. I know too, from meetings with lone fathers, that this same – but opposite – frustration applies to them with such as icing birthday cakes, tacking up hems, sewing on name-tapes. Linear parents so often feel relegated to the company of their own gender.

We may look self-contained and bossy: we may cope with house and children, garden, a full-time job, maybe run the local Gingerbread and give talks to the Parents' Association; but underneath all that superb efficiency lurks a disappointingly under used libido. This is frequently at the root (perhaps even subconsciously) of much early one-parent unhappiness. Self-pity creeps through the merest chink and at certain phases of the moon an unstoppable frustration builds up.

How many of us have cold-bloodedly accepted the putting up of shelves, painting of ceilings, fixing of stair-carpets in exchange for a night's lodging? For, it must be said, we miss out, and mind missing out, on sex.

There's no pat answer: obviously one cannot conjure up a lover from empty air. On the other hand, under certain conditions there seems no point in turning down chances. 'It is a tough world for us,' writes one divorced mother, 'and a happy relationship with a man, even if very brief, can change the whole tenor of one's life and leave one with marvellous renewed energy. It's the physiological as well as the mental unwinding. Very different from the sex-taken-for-granted of my married days.' How one learns to appreciate the physical. Learns, too, to throw off the too-perfect contention that it is impossible to make love to anyone unless you intend to feel deeply for ever and for evermore. One can. Sometimes one ought.

I know that certain one-parents experience a sense of guilt

about having any sex life at all. Some actually feel humiliated, others affronted, when a man makes a pass. It's fairly common to find mothers afraid of being thought promiscuous, particularly women who never have been married and who may possibly feel the very existence of their child labels them 'easy'. It has been suggested, too, that a Triangular-family woman may see any lone mother as a direct threat to her own husband. Some imagine that unattached women are invariably wanting – or, worse, needing – sex. In fact, like everyone else, the desire in us comes and goes. It is not a gnawing presence.

If possible try to get a couple of nights away sometimes. Another Gingerbread parent might well agree to take over on a reciprocal arrangement. It's a much better plan than trying to smuggle a man upstairs when the children are asleep. They are never asleep.

A series of 'uncles' is a sad business too. One uncle can prove very satisfactory to the entire family; but start ringing the changes and parental authority begins to sink into a state of distrust and confusion.

To the old question: Can you live without it? Well, yes, obviously you can. But I doubt that one's a better person physically, mentally or emotionally for such abstinence. If religious leanings or moral self-pressure come down against it – and your conscience would warp if you gave in – for your own peace of mind and body, then don't. Like smoking or drinking or chocolate, the longer the gap between giving it up and the present moment the less personally important the subject becomes. One graduates.

While on the subject of sex it is impossible to separate events from the tangible presence of children. It's a solemn fact that having children in the house with no resident second parent restricts not only one's broader social life, it more or less curtails one's sex life. With tiny children, all right. Once they become both mobile and attention-binding, it is less plain sailing.

Father alone

100,000 families in Britain are motherless

Relatively few men are given care and control of children in contested cases, though such a phenomenon is by no means unknown. Only infrequently does a father start off into one-parenting on a basis of fear and anxiety – the 'snatch-back' neurosis or the sickening worry of whether care and control proper will ultimately be granted.

Most men left holding the baby are in that position because their wives left both them and the children simultaneously, be it through death, desertion, long-term hospitalization or (very occasionally) prison sentence. Fathers seldom have any positive choice about taking on the children – they're landed (albeit happy to be landed). No man, either, shares our female opportunities of electing independently to construct a one-parent family from scratch.

Public opinion is – and always has been – more sympathetic towards a father left with the children than to a mother in the same rocky boat. Neighbours bake pies, wash woollens, undertake limited baby-minding. Social services are more likely to conjure up ways and means of enabling a father to carry on with a full-time job. Some go-ahead areas run a 24-hour 'relief mother' scheme which, in that period of readjustment between functioning as a two-parent family and floating satisfactorily in the Linear, can sometimes actually avoid the crisis of children being taken into care.

The greater part of society, even now, does not expect a man to brush the stairs, mix the batter, hang out the smalls, expect even less that he should tackle the nursery chores: nappies, bathing, preparing milk mixtures, feeding and winding. He is not thought capable of working out weaning schedules, coping with minor ailments, clearing up sick, visiting the children's wear department to buy the next size up in Babygro. And this fixed attitude can be most irritating for any father determined to make a go of mothering in addition to his paternal role.

He must not appear ungrateful in the face of unsolicited gifts of fruit cake, nor must he snap at the friend who recommends a change of milk formula for the baby who is perfectly content with his present feeds. The battling lone father must contrive to sit fairly neatly in the cleft stick of, on the one hand, feeling he's going to be offered assistance if he *asks* for it, and, being allowed to carry on without interference so long as he's doing all right.

It's tempting to label persistent angels of mercy as meddlers, but don't let them nettle you as much as they did one father who, when informed that his ten-year-old was helping the neighbour to make biscuits, which he'd be bringing home for tea, responded with, 'Damn you! If we want biscuits we'll bloody well go and buy them!' Remember, when you feel like saying 'damn you' to patronizing acquaintances – bite your coated tongue before you do. You never know, one day your domestic sanity may hang upon their aid. Be diplomatic.

Along with the widely held belief that Linear fathers are either incapable or unwilling to take on the meaner jobs connected with home and children, runs the more daunting concept that all men (whether anybody's father or not) should 'go out to work' regardless of personal commitments.

A man newly responsible for the sole charge of his children must weigh up the odds of going out to work – with the back-up of child-minder or nursery (even though he might feel happier looking after those children himself) – as against giving up his job and thus acquiring something of a stigma as a man unemployed by choice. Certainly any father who opts to 'do right' by his children must also be prepared, in some measure, to shrug off the opinions of the righteous.

The single father is, in law, every bit as entitled to stay at home, with Supplementary Benefit the sole means of support, as is any single mother. Any Social Security officer who infers that such a man ought to get his thumb out is overstepping his authority. Some do. There is no obligation for any single parent (of either sex) to register as available for work, as long as he is physically caring for at least one school-aged child.

However, common practice swings the other way. Most lone fathers choose to turn down this DHSS offer. Work preserves his independence, even though his earning capacity is often enormously cut back. Cut back because:

(a) he must necessarily pay out for child-minders;
(b) he must generally forget about being able to put in for overtime and weekend work;
(c) any type of shift work is incompatible with reasonable expectations of daily-helps, child-minders, and nurseries.

The loss of one adult mouth to feed in no way financially compensates for extra expenditure involved, because children with only one (working) parent are inevitably more expensive to run, *per capita*, than are those with a second parent ready to fill in all gaps.

In spite of the Equal Opportunities Act and the principle of fair play for all, the fact remains that men in full-time work still earn more, generally, than women in full-time work: thus we find a greater proportion of single fathers opt to remain in employment. The pay angle is reflected in numbers of lone parents claiming Family Income Supplement from the DHSS: 1 per cent of fathers to 30 per cent of mothers.

I don't know whether it's pride or reticence or neither, but the sort of mateyness one finds between single mothers doesn't seem to operate on the same spontaneous system between single fathers. Men would rather pay for work done, on the whole, than cooperate in swap schemes. It's so much easier to ask again, they claim, if the favour's on a commercial footing. Nevertheless, they'd do well to make themselves known to the local Gingerbread, if only to use it as a safety-valve against possible isolation, as a fount of relevant information, as action-stations in a family emergency. There's no obligation to join the social junketings of the group, though the children would obviously enjoy mixing.

Fathers often maintain that they feel inhibited when it comes to approaching organizations specifically set up to help single parents (could this be some latent hang-up about 'the unmarried *mother*' and her child?) as they feel they'll be swamped by female concern and help. Not at all. Though most single parents are women it doesn't follow that all who work on their behalf are also women. Most of the legal advice available through organizations is offered by male lawyers and a good deal of the welfare help too. When caught in a fog of legal, practical, emotional or child-orientated problems never be afraid – lone fathers – to use these services. Neither do the local social workers imagine you have to be down-and-out in order to warrant their attention.

One lone father I spoke to contacted his area's *Townswomen's Guild* and asked whether any housebound member would – for a small fee – take on the family mending and knitting. He was put in touch with a stout middle-aged lady who has become the loved 'auntie' of his two little girls. He takes this acquaintance further and says, 'We all feel easy with Gwen. I mean, she didn't come poking into our lives like a welfare woman, trying to do good. She never makes herself obtrusive; never does more than I ask her to do, so I'm not beholden to her. She accepts payment for what she does without any embarrassment.

It was the deal, after all, wasn't it? I find that I want to talk to her a lot about the girls' upbringing. I need a woman's advice on all sorts of things. Sex, for instance. I don't mind telling you, I'm scared stiff of answering the inevitable questions when they become teenagers and all that. They get lessons on it at school, but it's not quite the same as being able to ask questions privately, is it? If we still know Gwen when they're big enough to understand, I'll get her to explain to them, show them how to manage ... she's that sort of an easy person.'

Country fathers could try such as the local *Women's Institute* on a similar tack or any other likely clique where there are women who may have time to spare.

See Appendix

Cruse

Gingerbread Advice

Marriage Guidance Council

Mothers' Union

NACRO

National Council for the Divorced and Separated

National Council for One Parent Families

National Federation of Solo Clubs

National Society for the Prevention of Cruelty to Children

Parents' Anonymous

Parents Without Partners

Samaritans

Vineyard Project

10 Putting your house in order

A social worker, generally a sensible woman, once roundly rebuked me for expressing concern about the children should I have the misfortune to die before they grew up. I had, in fact, actually woken the previous night to worry mildly: What *would* happen if I died?

'What do you mean, *if* you died? We'll all die.'

'I meant ...' and she knew it, 'what happens if I pop off soonish?'

'Nobody's indispensable,' she stated, flatly.

'Oh no?' I couldn't help muttering, 'not even the single parent?' But she was already explaining, detached as a textbook...

'... a recognized symptom of a woman approaching breaking-point, imagining the world won't be able to carry on without her. And the interesting point is that it's just that type of woman ...' here she fixed me with a steely eye, 'who seems compulsively to take on more and more work, as though to ensure that at least she'll leave some unfinished chore behind her.' Freud was it? Or whom? I didn't much care.

'Balls!' I said: and I never use the word. 'It's nothing more nor less than a guilty conscience making itself felt as I fall into middle-age.' For, with all my brood, with all that stretch of one-parenting behind me, I'd not till that point given any thought either to making a will or appointing guardians. And never once had any form of life assurance crossed my otherwise clear mind. All I'd done in preparation for the great change-over was to fill in a form for the Anatomist General stating that he was welcome to my earthly remains.

Until we pull our thumbs out and act none of us has any claim at all to a tranquil night's sleep: it serves us right if we're badgered by the recurring question ... 'What happens if ... ?' We have to face the possibility. It is recklessly improper to adopt total optimism in such a context, lunatic to toss our all into the levelling lap of the state. We must 'make provision'. Provision both physical and financial.

Some sort of *life insurance* is a sensible start. Life *assurance* actually. And there are several varieties to choose from.

An *endowment policy* is particularly relevant to the one-parent family. Fix upon a period of so many years ahead, taking into account your own age and the ages of the children: say fifteen, twenty, twenty-five years. Then resolve the sum of money ultimately figuring. Two thousand? Three? Ten? More? And what happens is this: every year you pay your premium and for that you get what might be termed a double option: either, at the end of the fixed period you receive the lump sum (nicely in time for children going to college, getting married, needing to be bailed out?), or, if you die, even be it half-an-hour after taking out the policy, that same enormous sum materializes. But that glittering pile is regarded in law as part of your estate, and as such is eligible for *Capital Transfer Tax*. Thus, left without safeguard, the children would still miss out, so, with the help of solicitor or bank manager organize a *Trust Fund*. Appoint trustees who, after your death, will administer this particular plum entirely in the children's favour in terms of maintenance allowances, school fees, holidays, even mortgage repayments where relevant. Banks readily undertake trustee-ships and their charges are not steep. A solicitor is not such a good idea: solicitors, too, are mortal and a change in mid-stream may not entirely suit the children's lot. Of course any reliable and reasonably intelligent lay person may be nominated trustee, but be sure he really *is* concerned for the children, that he has adequate time to administer the Trust and that he is not too old. The last being on earth to be appointed trustee is the prospective guardian (whom we shall come to in a minute) for, if suddenly inhabited by a bad spirit, he could well turn this supposedly protected money to his own account.

An *income protection policy* is another good buy for the single-parent. It is also probably the cheapest, and it does just what its title suggests. It assures a fixed income for the children – should you die – over a given number of years. Thus, if you elect to take out a policy to cover a period of twenty-five years, but you die after only two, then the insurance company will pay an annual sum (£1,000, £2,000 ... whatever you arranged) for the next twenty-three years. However, if you live for twenty years after taking out the policy, then the money will only be paid for five years, and so on. If, as you doubtless hope, the passage of twenty-five years still sees you hale and hearty, then you've gambled the luck of living against the loss of your premiums. It's all gone. But, after all, you're still about.

So, where ought we to buy this life assurance? How do we differentiate between the good buy and the bad risk? And who are those door-to-door insurance men? Ought one to invite them in for a cup of coffee?

First, we must buy from a reputable *broker* (look in the Yellow Pages). He will be able to advise on particular policies best suited to a given situation taking into account present and predictable income, age, ages and number of children and (important) state of policy-holder's health. (Look to your weight.) The door-to-door agent or salesman is acting only for a single company, so lacks the wide choice of policies open to a broker. The door-to-door men may, indeed, have very little knowledge of any wider implications of insurance. No, then, do not invite the nice man in for a cup of coffee, not even if you haven't spoken to a soul bar the children all day.

Appointing a guardian: there are three ways of doing this; by will, by deed, or by application to the court. It's probably unnecessary to say that nobody must be put up as prospective guardian without his/her express consent: certain people, after all, may not be thrilled to open their post to find they've inherited half-a-dozen children.

By will. When one parent in a Triangular Family dies, the other automatically becomes legal guardian of any legitimate children of the union. Where parents are divorced and the one with custody of the children dies, the remaining parent may then apply to the court for guardianship and care. However, this guardianship by the hitherto 'absent' parent may be tempered by the terms of a mother's (father's) will. This could name an additional person as joint guardian, and the surviving parent must abide by this arrangement.

Where there is no 'absent' parent, then the mother (father) must indicate whom she intends to appoint. No guardian, incidentally, need also accept care and control. A solicitor, for example, may be asked to serve as guardian, while a godmother

133

or aunt might be responsible for day-to-day welfare.

By deed. This is quite separate from the parent's will, and is a formal statement drawn up clearly appointing one or two guardians. It is signed before a witness under seal. Legal direction is essential, but is not in this instance expensive.

By court order. In the absence of other guardianship arrangements a court may appoint one upon application. An additional guardian may also be appointed, to work with the person named by the late parent. This is more likely in cases where a particular child requires very special care or guidance (if handicapped, sick, emotionally or socially 'difficult'), or where the new guardian is in some way inadequate.

Any proportion of money left to the child (with the exception of Trust money) either by his parents or by anybody else, may be withdrawn by the guardian for that child's material support. (That statement alone should indicate the importance of choosing the right person.) Or, if the child has inherited nothing of much moment the guardian can claim a weekly maintenance from the state. This allowance goes on until the child is nineteen, or later if he continues in full-time education. You can get details of this scheme from any DHSS office.

Where money is in short supply a guardian may like to consider taking out a personal *Protection Policy*, with the children named as beneficiaries. The guardian assures his/her life for a given sum and a given number of years. If the guardian should die within that period the sum assured is paid out. If he survives, however, then nothing is forthcoming and the policy ceases. Under such a scheme premiums may be payable from money left to the children or through a Trust Fund, if any, so long as the children remain sole beneficiaries.

Making a will Even if you're under the impression that you own nothing of value it really is terribly urgent that you make a will. It needn't cost you more than a sheet of writing paper. And, even if the children only inherit your record-player, a little pile of paste jewellery and 'the residue of the estate' (which means everything else you own at the time – kitchen pans, bedding, books, rugs, each item down to half-pots of marmalade and worn out cardigans) then at least they're legally entitled to lay their little hands on these nondescript trappings. Otherwise, in the case of a person who is separated but not legally divorced, the ex-spouse has every right (over and above the children) to claim everything up to the value of £8,750, whether cash, kind or property. For most of us that would, indeed, mean the lot.

A simple will is the sort you can dash out at home. However, if it's going to be treated as a valid document there are four points to remember:

1 You must make it abundantly clear that this piece of writing is a will. Put down your full name and the date on which you're making it. Then, if you've ever made one before but can't get hold of it to destroy it, state that you 'revoke' all former wills.

2 You appoint an executor (executrix if female) who is a person who sees that the terms of your will are obeyed and actually arranges the handing out of belongings, money and/or property to the right people.

3 List all items you want to leave to specific people. But think ahead ... you may exchange many major items several times before you die (typewriter, sewing machine and so on), so word it absolutely that you leave so-and-so 'the sewing machine I own at the time of my death'. Wills are interpreted with the most finicky exactitude, so beware. After special bequests leave 'the residue' to either one or more people. But don't set up obvious quarrels.

4 Get the thing witnessed. Anyone may do this (except a blind person), but he must be someone who isn't going to benefit. Witnesses ought to be eighteen or over, though if there's honestly nobody within range then a minor will be tolerated. No wife or husband of a witness may inherit unless they marry *after* the will is drawn up.

Witnesses, by the way, don't necessarily need to read the contents of a will. What they must see is you signing it, then add their signature under yours, with address and occupation. That's all.

Make certain that you keep this document safely, and for heaven's sake tell two or three people (who are likely to live longer than you are) where it is. Any bank will keep it for you, or a solicitor. If it can't be found after you die, then your estate is divided up as though no will had ever been made.

A more complicated will really ought to have the finger of a solicitor upon it. Where, for instance, there are a good many separate 'parcels' of relatively valuable land/houses/antiques, etc., or where a mortgage is involved or a family house to be divided between X number of offspring. No solicitor will charge all that much for doing a will, but you can't get it on Green Form.

Changes may be made (codicils, they're called) but be sure to add them at the end (not, for instance in the margin or by crossing out and substituting). Each codicil must be witnessed as with the main will, and the date of the change (not of the original) added clearly.

If you do die without drawing up a will you will have 'died intestate' and it will cause your children a lot of hassle.

National Insurance No contributions are compulsory while you are still married, even if you are no longer living with your husband. A separation by Court Order still leaves you 'married', thus benefiting under your husband's contributions. However, with divorce you are considered a person in your own right and must pay insurance rates according to one of several codes. The sum varies with your position as an employed person, a self-employed person or a non-employed person. If your income is abysmally low you may be exempted from making any contributions at all. Obtain all individual advice from the DHSS. But don't delay after the decree is granted, or you may find yourself making up lost insurance payments. Knowledgeable solicitors will advise you to consider National Insurance contributions when the question of maintenance is raised.

Tax As a single householder you are now taxed on your own, that is no longer as an appendage to your husband's annual Return. Our income is less and our responsibility greater than hitherto, thus comparatively few of us pay any income tax at all.

We are entitled to the same tax relief as a married man (i.e. single person's relief plus additional relief for being in sole charge of child/children).

A father paying maintenance under a court order may deduct tax at the standard rate before that money reaches his ex-wife/child unless the amount involved is pretty small. If yours comes through thus depleted a claim must be made to retrieve this tax from the Inland Revenue. Do this when filling in your

Return. Nothing comes automatically: if you don't take the initiative you may well miss out.

Tax relief may also be claimed on mortgage repayments as long as they are met from your own money (not, I mean, if your ex-husband pays them on your behalf).

Widow's Benefit is taxed, with the exception of that part of it intended as children's maintenance.

Educational awards and grants are not taxed.

I've always found people at our local Inland Revenue Office very sympathetic and helpful. They are used to coping with the bemused public, so a foggy-minded single-parent is given a patient hearing. If not clear about your tax entitlements or liabilities don't hesitate to carry your problems to their door.

See Appendix

Anatomist General

Association of Widows in Great Britain

Child Poverty Action Group

Cruse

DHSS

Fifth Demand Group

Rights of Women

11 Social life: holidays

One day, with a doomlike thud, you may realize that you're unable to go out. You are not suffering from agoraphobia: nothing as constricting. You just don't want to go out because, even if you have plenty of cash for baby-sitters, you simply cannot face people on a socializing level any more. A sort of public paralysis. It's bad.

This is partly laziness, partly our practical facility for making excuses, mostly perhaps a dread of experiencing – again – that awful hollow feeling of being alone in a crowd. The safe pleasures of our circumscribed family lives seem too good to leave.

The contented solitary seldom worries about 'meeting new people': she doesn't want to. She doesn't see that it matters. Yet her protecting shell may crack after the children have grown up and left home, when her own company is all there is. Yet the kind of social life available to the average single parent can be a bit odd. Being without a partner guarantees one's position as odd-man-out, thus difficult to fit in at the dinner table. We are paired off with aged cousins of our host, with nervous young men lately released from hospital or with teenaged sons of the family, who only talk of motorbikes and O-levels.

The good hostesses, perhaps our well-intentioned friends, care terribly about our future. Or they just like matchmaking. They rake out eligible greying bachelors of doubtful inclination, widowers well out of mourning (generally with children or housekeeper trouble), and divorced men ready after a decent interval to take on another woman. There is always a certain embarrassment about these throwings-together. You have been told, 'I've found a marvellous man you must meet!' and doubtless he has been similarly primed to endure a complementary marvel. In any event, the good old reserve is well spread before you utter so much as a how-d'you-do. Disappointment is usually mutual. The one turns out plain and serious to the point of gloom, able only to converse upon the subjects of euthanasia and abortion – the other music-hall bald with onions on his breath, a teller of jokes and a huge laugher. Visibly each springs away into the private recesses of an unlistening mind. The flop is total: the return to solitude pure balm.

This is not so balmy, though, for the children. If 'family' is to prove the be-all-and-end-all of social interchange they're going to find their horizons uncommonly limited.

'We don't know anybody!' is the wail of more than one Linear child. Extend this cry to lack of holidays (and 32 per cent of one-parent families never have a holiday) and a quick check on how many relatives were 'lost' with family break-up, and you should experience a really shattering propulsion into the regions of self-therapy. Escape into the world one must, if only as an adjunct to the children. Absolute withdrawal is a luxury we cannot, for their sake, afford. Nor must we get into a habit of perpetually blaming the chores for grabbing our free time.

The more immediate outings and treats are dependent upon this new resolution as much as on cash. There are still an enormous number of excursions to be had for free – especially in London. An eye to the local paper or a small investment in the shape of a 'Where to go' type booklet (*Kids' London*, for instance) can help start you off. Make use, too, of the free public library, record library, toy library, but be careful not to let your tickets get overdue or you'll be in for a fine. Take the children (don't send them) to all museums, ancient monuments and open spaces within cheap and easy reach. Don't refuse them the opportunity of school outings: if you honestly can't afford them, then ask for financial help from the Education Department, Social Services, Parent–Teacher Association.

Real go-away holidays are, if not actually essential, almost as necessary as summer itself. And don't get hooked on the idea that you have to go far. It may sound corny and old-fashioned, but what really puts the spark into a holiday is change. Change more than rest. And, though it is hard to scrape together enough money when our living hovers at Social Security level or below, a real holiday in strange beds needn't be a dream, it can be experienced. By lowering our sights to a swap, a hostel or even a working holiday, that change can be accomplished. There are grants to be had if one learns where to beg, so the daunting cost of public transport needn't be totally off-putting.

And while touching on transport: never just go and buy a railway ticket straight. There are so many cheap bargains – not always very well advertised – and it's often possible to travel far more cheaply than you imagined. Pre-booked mid-week journey returns are *half* the normal fare, for instance. Then, throughout the summer, there's generally an 'Awayday' offer enabling accompanied children to travel for next to nothing. Promotion drives, too, in connection with some consumer commodity, will periodically offer free tickets (anywhere in Britain, including Sealink) in exchange for saved vouchers. Keep your eyes open.

One mother, having dutifully gone away to the seaside with her two toddlers, returned vowing never to take a 'lone' holiday again. She had rented a cottage not exactly remote, but not in a commercially holiday-orientated area – and had found the locals insular and the weather British.

'For the first time since my marriage broke up I missed having another person to share with,' she explained. 'At heart I missed being two people instead of one. Somehow it's different at home, but away, always conscious of having to make it a good time for the little boys, everything fell flat. I wanted to come back after only a couple of days.'

If she'd contemplated combining with another Linear Family she might well have felt differently. One can either find a sharing family through personal advertising, or through one of the few organizations which concentrate on that type of break.

Gingerbread Holidays, sometimes in conjunction with area Social Services, provide both two-family shares and group holidays. The function of the first scheme is to introduce families with common interests, so that in many cases they can plan their own holidays together: Youth Hostelling, camping, fruit-picking or whatever. The second is aimed at perhaps less adventurous families who prefer to join in with a wider crowd: a block booking of chalets, caravans, camping space or holiday camp accommodation is earmarked for one-parent families over given dates. The criteria governing choice rest with value for money, and help with costs may be forthcoming if your coffers are wretchedly low. Ask about this help when you make initial inquiries.

Singlehanded runs a Holiday Service. Again, it's a sharing system using selected hotels where families with similar interests and backgrounds may combine forces. Ages of children are also taken into account. Group holidays of the 'homely' type are arranged for unaccompanied children too.

Though holidays abroad are generally out as far as we are concerned, *One Parent Family Holidays (Continental)* are doing their best to push us up into the migratory bracket. As many as 250 single parents and children have participated in a joint holiday over a half-term holiday in Majorca; as few as twenty have escaped to Morocco in October. There's no attempt to 'partner' people, and everybody is free to join in planned activities and tours or neither, as they wish.

This same agency will also help parents, with or without their children, to arrange short breaks in Paris, Brussels, Bruges, Amsterdam and The Hague. Costs are always kept at minimum-for-value.

Large commercial travel firms often make a child-fare reduction when *two* adults are booking a holiday flight, which is a drawback if no second parent is available. *Thomson's* and *British Airways Enterprise* are, so far as I know, the only agencies which reduce child-fare one-to-one with each full-fare adult. It is, then, almost always more economical to book continental holidays through a specialist organization geared specifically to one-parent needs.

The National Council and *Gingerbread Holidays* both keep registers of families, one-parented or two-parented, who offer holiday accommodation either on an exchange basis or simply as visiting space. So does *The National Foster Care Association*: *Cruse* (widows only) too. You don't have to live at the seaside, near mountains, beside lakes or even deep in the country to offer your house either as a swap or open-house. Some families actually want to take a holiday in Wolverhampton.

When cash is really tight, yet the need for a break is getting to the point of rather more than shortage of temper, then see about getting yourself nose-dived into the 'needy' section. Local authorities (Social Services) are empowered under the *Public Health Act 1968* to supplement holiday costs for parents under stress. The local Education Department should also be able to provide assistance towards holiday expenses. Ask.

Most of the big *voluntary societies* run schemes whereby

needy families benefit by means of holiday grants or by the provision of caravans and flatlets where parents and children may go for a few days. It's worth applying to any local charities too: philanthropical societies and so on or maybe the local Round Table. Try.

If, because of work or because without conscience you can admit to needing a rest from the children, it would be worth trying for a holiday for them, without you. No need to go for the expensive 'adventure' type of holiday one sees advertised in the Sunday papers: a lot of children don't particularly want organized adventure. None of mine would step into a canoe if you paid them. *Children's Country Holidays Fund* and the WRVS each run similar schemes for sending unaccompanied children into the countryside or seaside for a fortnight, usually during August. You provide the pocket money, and make a small contribution towards costs, otherwise the break is covered by voluntary contributions.

The great thing is, somehow, to heave oneself and one's children out of the isolation rut. Make a list; lay a plan, promise yourselves a holiday – either together or apart – and work towards it. Pull all the stops out.

We invariably set off on holiday during the closed season. Sometimes we even manage to fit in two breaks a year – one in March or April, one in October. You can only do this, of course, when the children are pre-school or still at primary (where it is acceptable to go absent on account of family holidays). There are many advantages for the outdoor-hearty and for those who prefer room to move and can tolerate winds. Holiday cottages and flats are very cheap out-of-season (catch them in early October till just before Easter). The beaches are deserted and full of lost pails left by the summer folk. There are no queues at the ferries, no crushes in the shops. All but the minimum of resort specialities (hot-dog stalls, bingo, dodgems, laughing policemen) are shrouded for the winter, yet one can still track down those two essentials to any child-geared holiday – ice-cream and lettered rock. In short, off-season is cheap. For any self-sufficient family (or two families together) the grey sea and pale sunshine can be every bit as enjoyable as the press and heat of summer. There are generally good travel concessions (British Rail) through the winter months if you look for them.

The most important thing to remember is to take masses of changes of clothes. Whatever the temperature somebody is going to fall in. Anoraks, scarves, woollen hats, wellies and masses of socks. Hot water bottles too.

See Appendix

Children's Country Holidays Fund

Cruse

Dr Barnardo's

Gingerbread

Gingerbread Holidays

Mothers' Union

National Council for One Parent Families

National Federation of Solo Clubs

National Foster Care Association

National Society for Mentally Handicapped Children

One Parent Holidays (Continental)

Singlehanded

Singles Holidays

Toc H

Women's Royal Voluntary Service

Youth Hostels Association

12 Adding to the one-parent family

Women whose maternal instincts run dizzily high often make bad wives. This isn't a contradiction in terms. We are occasionally so cock-a-hoop with motherhood that there simply isn't room for a man, not, anyway, a resident full-time man. I strongly suspect that a goodly proportion of deliberate single-parents stem from marriages which fail subsequent to this child-concentration. The adored children become those unwitting birds who toss the husband out of the nest. Taking this mothering syndrome one step further, it could happen that the existing children of such a one-parent family prove insufficient in number.

The urgent call generally comes in spring as nature intended, and the need to expand seems imperative. Our maternal nerve-ends twitch for another baby, and given adequate housing and finance there is no reason on earth why this infant should not happen. The conventional Triangular Family is by no means essential to the heralding in of new blood.

There are three main approaches:

1 Personally giving birth

2 Single-parent adoption

3 Fostering, either long- or short-term

Over a series of fertile springs I have joyfully subscribed to all these methods.

Illegitimacy is no longer considered particularly improper, and the deliberately planned single-parent baby is a ratification of our time. Certainly the processes of pregnancy and parturition are no more necessarily fraught than in two-sided reproduction: there is just a matter of more concentrated responsibility to take up. Somebody said there were no illegitimate children, only illegitimate parents. I would suggest that illegitimacy exists only in the opinion of the individual – a narrow individual.

Indeed, the National Council will not tolerate the word at all. For them a child is either 'born in wedlock' or 'out', both being equally legal. A baby, breathing and in every way existing, cannot *per se* be irregular.

However, to practical matters. Being pregnant on your own, with other children to look after, may be a bit of a strain. Weigh up your own mental and physical stamina and look backwards objectively at past pregnancies before you start another one. Think about who's going to look after the other children when you are in hospital. This may be a mere forty-eight hours; it may be a full ten days. In any case, be prepared to lay on adequate and loving substitute care, even if you are lucky enough to find a doctor who's still in favour of home delivery. I used a super foster-mother, recommended by Social Services, to take over while I gave birth to my last daughter. The children visited her several times before they moved in and the whole event went off like a holiday. They even returned home with new vests as proxy mum had faintly disapproved of their filigree cast-downs. It's unlikely, though, that the Social Services will concur to foot the bill for this type of one-off fostering, especially considering the independent nature of the impending birth.

Older children, teenagers especially, need their opinions taking seriously. The newly adult can be hugely censorious. Indeed, I go so far as to maintain that much adolescent permissiveness exists only in the mind of those who wish to peddle it. My eldest child was six when I last gave birth, so everything was easy. As far as he was concerned mothers had babies and I happened to be having one. We could all look forward to it. But I wouldn't try it now however strong the personal temptation. I ask my teenagers today and at first they hoot derisively but when pressed for a sensible reaction they admit the situation would be embarrassing, perhaps even shaming and they would wish me to keep indoors like Queen Victoria for the entire nine months. I suspect there is also fear, for the teenager, of a man getting a foothold in the family, of tranquil self-government undermined.

The *Maternity Grant*, a lump sum, is available to all mothers who have paid at least twenty-six weeks' insurance contributions. This money is essentially for baby needs like nappies, layette, carricot and so on. And remember that baby equipment and clothing can be bought second-hand at a fraction of 'new' cost. Personally, as you may have already gathered, I swear by Oxfam as their wares are clean and their assistants – if you dare call such cashmered ladies so – take infinite trouble to cooperate. They will, for instance, put your name down for the next decent crib to come in. My last one was a vast bassinet in immaculate order, almost given to me.

The single mother is, obviously, just as entitled to *Maternity Allowance* as is the double mother. Insurance contributions again provide the criteria upon which this eleven-weeks-before and seven-weeks-after payment is made.

See leaflet BM4, obtainable from Welfare Clinic, Post Office or local DHSS for all current details of these two benefits. Claims should be sent to the DHSS.

Job protection If you're in full-time employment and have been in the same job for a minimum of two years by the time Maternity Allowance is payable (approximately eleven weeks before the birth), your employer is obliged by law to keep the job open for you. You must be prepared to return to work at the beginning of the eighth week after the baby is born.

No woman, of whatever status, may now be sacked from any job for the sole reason of pregnancy.

Adoption There is no legal bar to a single person – man or woman – adopting a child. There is, however, a shortage of adoptable babies, and obviously the childless Triangular Family gets priority over the burgeoning single parent. Nevertheless, there's no harm in asking for an infant. Once you move upwards from infant level, chances brighten. The two/three/four-year-old can sometimes find himself on the shelf. It is, of course, harder work. The child comes in with his own established speech pattern and mannerisms (normally an essential part of 'family'), his own ideas about life and contact and behaviour; his own character neatly tied up. He is *not* going to pass as a little offshoot of yourself for some time to come (nor, necessarily, at all), for his progress, his 'copying', by which all children learn the basics, has been previously mapped out to another scale.

I have twice adopted four-year-olds. The girl was quiet,

fastidious, withdrawn, too-good-to-be-real; the boy obstreperous, rude, dirty, loving, physical. At a rough look-back I'd say that it took about two years in each case before either child really belonged in the fullest sense. They have both retained, beneath the marks which identify them as a true part of our own family, many of their pre-adoption characteristics. The girl, for instance, does not easily show emotion nor does she like discussing school work, activities with friends and so on. She is still largely a secret-guarding child. The boy, quite opposite, positively wears his feelings for all to see: love, hate, anger, excitement, surliness, every phase is given full treatment. So, in taking on an adoptive child singlehanded, one must be prepared to recognize the type of character inherent in that two/three/four-year-old (or older) and weigh up one's own abilities to cope with it. For one-parenting a newly-introduced child is an exacting, sometimes exhausting, frustrating, agonizing job, calling for full play of maternal cunning.

Neither of my adopted children had previously lived in a family, and residential care, however excellent (and certainly in the boy's case it was excellent), does little to prepare the child for the real world. The child must come to terms with his new circumstances: the withdrawal of routine, the acceptance of one constant adult in place of on-duty-off-duty nurses, the business of considering others instead of fighting your way to the top of the heap or lying, unprotesting, at the bottom.

One rule I'd apply pretty stringently, in fairness to existing children of the family, is that the newcomer must be younger than the present youngest. He must also be approved by his potential brothers and sisters.

We all went down to the nursery to visit David before he came to us; spent half a day there, had lunch with him, played with him, started to get to know him. If any of my children had felt he wasn't the one for us I would have done some serious thinking. Luckily the essential spark of instant loving was there, so, in spite of all, he joined the tribe.

Every Social Services Department must, under the 1975 *Children's Act*, run an adoption section. Yet it is still comparatively rare for single parents to adopt, possibly because most social workers feel that a two-parented family is more likely to give a rejected child the stability he needs. However, one could argue that as a quarter of all British marriages end in divorce, the background stability then collapses and one in four adopted children begins all over again as part of a Linear Family. Thus there must be an admitted risk, statistically speaking, in placing any child with a young couple who have been married for, say, five years or less. Now the single mother, more often the older single mother, is less likely to change her status by marrying subsequent to adopting. The stability of her family is ninety per cent certain. She is committed to mothering, not to mothering-plus-wifing.

On the whole it would seem that the more *outré* adopters are more fairly received by the large city boroughs or the national societies. There is no obligation to apply to your local Social Services Department, though it's likely that social workers from that office will be involved to some extent in the proceedings. And wherever you go it is likely that, should there be an available child, he will be offered to you for 'fostering with a view to adoption'. That's all right because they have to be sure. So do you. This does leave one with the option open, yet at the same time any chance of the child actually being removed is extremely slim. Many of us need months to decide, for the implications of taking on full moral, educational and financial responsibility for another little being are fairly staggering. While the child is fostered he receives a relatively adequate allowance: when legally adopted the full burden drops plumb into one's own tattered purse.

Although you must be over twenty-one (and the single parent in a position to expand her family is unlikely to be younger) there is, in fact, no legal upper limit beyond which you may not adopt. Pay no attention to those who tell you forty's the top: I was forty-four and practically penniless when I adopted David. My yardstick rests on the biological possibility of having my own child of similar age to the one taken in.

The necessary vetting process embraces at least one very thorough medical overhaul – both for mother and child, and also several inquisition-like interviews during which you must be prepared to bare the secrets of your heart and habits, and provide references from two trusty friends/employers/councillors/clergymen or whomsoever else you imagine might bear weight.

I experienced nothing but helpfulness and kindness from social workers toiling on my behalf. I never got the feeling that

I was considered eccentric or batty: never got the feeling, either, that they considered my existing children to be plenty without the addition of David. Judges, too, would appear to accept single-parent adoption without raising an eyebrow: after all, much investigation and testing of motives has gone into the new mother/new child relationship long before the matter is brought before the court. The child is obliged to live as part of the adopter's family for at least three months, often much longer, before the case can be heard, and by that time basic mutual testing and settling in has usually been accomplished.

'I don't see,' said the judge in David's case, 'why this shouldn't be a very happy little family.' Personally I would have qualified his use of the word 'little'. David came in as Number Six, and already Number Seven was with us on a long-term fostering basis. (Number Eight came later.)

About fifty 'single adoptions' are granted each year, and by this I mean the grafting on of children who are unrelated by blood to their new mothers (or, more rarely, fathers). Until recently it was fairly common practice for an unmarried girl to legally adopt her own child, thus rendering him legitimate. Yet we single women who adopt a child have, so to speak, legally acquired fatherless offspring. A sort of legitimate illegitimacy. Curious.

The heftiest argument against single adoption is the old chestnut about single-parents 'snatching' babies from the arms of would-be two-parents. This contention, as I think must already be clear, is without base. No adoption department will give a lone mother half a thought while double parents are available. It is the child who has been 'in care' for a long time – years perhaps, certainly in David's case since birth – and for whom conventional adopters have been sought in vain, who may find himself confronted by a ready-made half-family; a family whom he will learn to call his own. Here we come into the realms of the so-called 'hard to place' child. Physically or mentally handicapped, racially 'unmatched' to the majority or double adopters, one of several siblings needing to be placed together, or simply, 'too old' (over four).

Those who are anti one-parent adoption are keen, too, on drawing attention to the great questionmark of the future. With only one parent, what happens if that one-and-only expires, becomes chronically incapacitated, marries a man who 'can't take to' the child? The comfortable answer is, of course, that after the rigorous pre-adoption medicals, long-term health is pretty nicely assured. Nevertheless, accidents do happen, and the truth is that we simply have to take our chance with the rest. That we must make a will and appoint guardians is only common sense (for technicalities see chapter 10) and it is proper that older children are aware of the arrangements that have been made. They ought, clearly, to have some say in the choice of guardian, for even quite small children are capable of worrying about being bereft of home and hearth. Indeed, this theme is often of consummate interest to adolescents, and one of my own daughters admits to a recurring daydream in which, with me safely beneath the sod, she bravely tackles the entire family single-handed. (Sometimes I feel she can hardly wait.)

The greatest handicap to single adoption is, to my mind, the additional juggling with home and school hours in the business of making a living; for a child new to the family is even more in need of constant parenting than are those already part and parcel of the circus. The fact that I do freelance work from home (usually choosing work hours after the children are in bed) made my own particular adoptions relatively easy in this respect. The cost of harbouring an additional child – several hundreds of pounds a year – has to be found from somewhere. If we haven't got a private supply coming in, then we have to compensate by good honest toil. The authorities would never let us adopt if, for instance, we depended upon Social Security.

Fostering If you know, for any of dozens of reasons, that full-blown adoption is out of the question, yet you still suffer from a type of congenital broodiness, then fostering is worth consideration. Lots of single women register as foster parents, and thank goodness morals have changed enough (I don't mean sexual morals) to render it 'proper' to receive a decent allowance, or wage if you like, for the exacting job of caring for and loving someone else's child. 'Do-gooder' is a label I detest almost as much as the National Council detests 'illegitimate'. But 'altruism' is alive and well, and perfectly respectable. I make no bones at all about earning the bulk of our living by looking after other people's children. I like fostering, I'm an excellent mother, I need to earn my bread (all our breads) out of something I can do at home. It is thus only logical that I should air both my training and my inclination in this direction. As a foster mother I regard myself as an integral part of the Social Service Department. Naturally I work longer hours – all hours – than any normal social worker and receive less money. Yet, important beyond any other consideration, the job enables me to be a constant parent because the allowance tops up my income to a level at which I need not 'go out to work'. Having one's delicious cake and eating it too? True. Fostering has it all wrapped up for over-maternal one-parents. And it can be done on two bases:

Long-term means a placement of six or more months. Often this extends to 'whole childhood' thus the long-term child can genuinely become part of the family.

Short-term means a placement of less than six months. Sometimes these are emergency stops: a telephone call (some boroughs pay for telephone installation and cover rental) followed by a child at the door. More frequently gaps in family care occur while the mother is in hospital, homeless or simply unable to cope for a while. Short-term children are likely to have more behaviour problems than are long-term. This is not for the possessive type of single-parent.

Lone parents possessing appropriate training and/or experience may like to specialize. This, if one really accepts fostering as part of family income, pays more, as well as being more demanding. For instance, as well as being registered with our local Social Services and with one London borough, I'm also on call to the nearby branch of the Society for Mentally Handicapped Children. Children come to our home for holidays, for weekends, sometimes only for odd days, to give mothers and fathers a rest. I find that my own family is enormously co-operative in this venture, accepting the shortcomings and differences of our visitors with practical compassion.

Some areas run training schemes for 'professional' foster parents (single parents are not barred) who undertake the care of difficult teenagers. This can be really tough work and requires a certain strain of dedication: much depends, too, upon the attitude of your own children and the amount of time they still demand. Professional fostering carries a fairly high wage in addition to the maintenance allowance. The wage part is taxable.

Scholastic agencies are often able to put one in touch with

boarding-school children who need holiday accommodation. Advertising as a holiday home is another way of attracting attention, though no publication may accept a notice without the understanding that full name and address will appear with the advertisement. This is the law. Many newspapers also require a written recommendation from a family doctor in order to be sure of bona fide foster families. Also, if starting out as a private foster parent, you must let the local authority know of your intention at least two weeks before any child moves in, though obviously special understanding is exercised in the case of emergency placements. The big drawback to this school-holidays fostering is lack of real protection against non-payment. One simply has to be brave enough to ask for maintenance in advance – monthly or weekly according to length of stay. It's difficult to set out rules regarding fees. What I do is assess the amount of cash I'll need to physically support the child per week and multiply by three. It depends a little bit, too, on what sort of home you're able to offer: I mean, if you're all-electric and have to buy every morsel of food you swallow, if going out to play means a walk to the park instead of tumbling out into the shaggy back garden, then both finances and time are more heavily drained off. In that case charge more.

Never feel guilty about making money out of doing anything as agreeable as looking after children. Other people get paid for things they enjoy. Why not you?

See Appendix

Association of British Adoption and Fostering Agencies

Church of England Children's Society

Dr Barnardo's

Family Care

Life

Lifeline Pregnancy Care

Marie Stopes

National Children's Homes

National Foster Care Association

Parents for Children

Thomas Coram Foundation

13 The parsimonious one-parent

The managing single-parent is no more out on a limb, from a material point of view, than is any relatively impoverished Triangular Family. The differences actually lessen the more one delves: it's only on the wider scale that our dilemma shows up as so bad. Almost all of us are 'poor' (subsistence level or below) while only some of them are.

The following catalogue of penny-pinching ideas applies equally to the beggarly of all social categories, whether half or whole families.

You only need to subscribe to the ranks of the impecunious and the independent. It's helpful, too, if you're willing to substitute time for hard cash. If you've never struck the type of low that leaves you without anything for the next meal, then as a lone parent you're lucky. The void exists, and something as megalithic and inescapable as a quarterly electricity payment can crash-dive us into destitution. Right back at the beginning, for instance, before I developed my best one-parenting powers, we plucked and cooked pigeons that we found dead as I maintained that heat kills all known germs. I now qualify that viewpoint.

Living, substantially, drops into four easy groups: food, shelter and sundry furnishings, clothes, and energy for light, heat, motion.

Expenses accorded to each can be hugely lessened by the employment of dodges and tricks, all perfectly honest, most perfectly tolerable.

Food must always be treated as potentially elastic. Go for nutritional value and bulk it out yourself rather than buy ready-mades. And avoid 'rubbish foods' which are largely composed of edible starch, sulphur dioxide, permitted emulsifiers, sodium aluminium silicate, saccharin, monosodium glutamate, stabilizers, colour, preservative and flavouring: they are expensive and provide empty calories.

Minced meat, that great standby of the British mother, can be doubled by adding oatmeal/rice/macaroni/noodles/bread-crumbs/stuffing-mix/diced potatoes or any other vegetable. It can be trebled by the further addition of dumplings or pie-crust top. It can be quadrupled if the pastry lies beneath as well as on top.

Pastry is an invaluable stretcher for dishes both savoury and sweet.

Soya bean is poor man's meat: excellent protein. Spun soya is available as a sort of false ham, beef, pork or natural (practically tasteless). Reconstitute and use as minced meat, or use half-and half with the real thing. Economical if bought in large packets from health shops or some grocers. Not economic if you get it in small sachets or ready-cooked in tins. The draw-back is that it causes wind.

Baked beans is another unsociable food, but high in protein again and children love it. It is cheap too and cheaper still if you make it yourself. Simple to prepare, especially if you have a solid fuel oven (long and slow) or pressure cooker. (If you haven't got a pressure cooker then it will save you pounds in the long run to put by for one now.)
To make baked beans:

Soak 450g (1 lb) haricot beans for around eight hours. Pour them into an earthenware/enamel pot (with lid) or a pressure cooker and add 2tsp mustard, 2tbs tomato puree, 60g (2oz) brown sugar and 2tbs each of golden syrup and black treacle. Cover with water so that no beans are poking out and stir in a large, chopped-up onion. Add a bayleaf and an odd bit of bacon fat/rind/bone if you have them. Cook overnight in the oven at a low temperature or about 1 hr in the pressure cooker. Renders the equivalent of eight to ten big-tins.

Sausage meat is cheaper weight-for-weight than sausages. Big sausages are cheaper weight-for-weight than chippolatas. But-chers' sausages by the string are cheaper weight-for-weight than wrapped, sterilized, supermarket ones. Sausage meat can be expanded in the same manner as minced meat (see above). Toad-in-the-hole is a way of making it more interesting and is one of the cheapest dishes of all.

Bones make excellent soups and stock by pressure cooking or long slow simmering on the lowest imaginable heat. Never throw away first-time-round bones; they're full of food value. Small children will gnaw them (better than a teething ring) though, as with dogs, avoid splintery chicken or lamb. Most butchers will give bones away, but don't expect them if you decline to buy anything else. Grocery counters often sport plastic parcels of bacon ribs at a few pence (for the baked bean pot). Once I had a neighbour who regularly brought over her weekend bones 'for the dog'. Always accept such bounty, but boil up the lot first for soup before extending generosity to any hound. Marrow bones (dirt cheap or free) are marvellous value and good occupational therapy for an inquiring toddler. Give him a narrow spoon or lolly stick with a cooked, cooled marrow bone and you've bought half-an-hour.

Fish is no longer cheaper than meat. Most small children don't like it all that much, especially as there are always bones. If chewed for long by a recalcitrant child fish turns to an unswallowable woolly mat: turn your own memory back and sympathize. Coley is often bought for middle-class cats. It is also delicious for the poor. Off-puttingly grey when raw it attains the look of decent cod with cooking, and tastes as good. Coley skin is positively abrasive, yet I have a small boy who invariably yells, 'Bags I the black stuff!' and downs it with rapture. Our fishmonger sometimes lets us have heads for 5p or so. Once, for rather more, we got a salmon head. Boil up this head and you'll get a mass of meat and stock. The liquid is so rich it turns glutinous when cold. Rice cooked up in this, with plenty of seasoning, makes a delicious meal.

Mammal heads become more grotesque the bigger they are. They are also very cheap, because nobody wants them except us. Concede to weakness only to the point of asking the butcher to cut out the eye (singular ... for half a pig's *tête* is enough at one time: think of your pan). Wash the whole thing under the cold tap without dwelling on its past, then quickly pack it into the pot or pressure cooker. Fill to one-third with water if in a pressure cooker, otherwise cover completely, add salt, bay, basil (anything you like except vegetables, which will turn sour if not eaten pretty quickly), and batten the lid. Simmer away for hours on next to no heat then pick all the bits of meat off the bone. Chop the more succulent salvage and stow it in a basin. Cover with skimmed stock and put it in the fridge. By tomorrow's lunch it will be brawn.

Tails and trotters are best for stock. Some clever people with terrific powers of divination manage to find nodules of meat on a pig's trotter. If you want to have a go cook it with a delicious sauce of brown sugar mixed with wine vinegar. My toddler likes to chew trotters.

Ox liver is the cheapest of all offal and is enormously rich in iron (magic for debilitated mums!). However, its flavour is a little fierce for young palates. Make it into liver pâté at a fraction of the price of the commercial equivalent. No need for a blender; a wooden spoon and a strong arm work as well, though slower to perfection. For five/six good helpings you'll need to mix up 225 g (½lb) lightly simmered (still pink) pounded/blended/minced ox liver, a cup of breadcrumbs, 60 g (2oz) butter or goodish margarine, 1tsp salt, a pinch of pepper, a small, finely chopped onion, a pinch or two of thyme or sage, and milk enough to make it all bind together. Push this mixture firmly down into a greased loaf tin, tie some foil or butter paper over its top, and bake in a slow oven for an hour. It is good hot or cold.

Bacon ends sell at a quarter the normal price, or less. If they're not displayed on the counter, ask. This is the only way we ever buy our bacon.

Cheeseparings emerge from the metaphor as real 'odds and ends' if you're pleasant to the grocer. He may charge you as much as half price: he may give them to you. Don't refuse, even if they're rock hard. These scraps grate down to provide the zip for a fine *gratin*. Often useless for eating uncooked.

Margarine is better for your arteries than butter, is cheaper (and more so if you buy those great square tubs), and it doesn't taste nasty, no matter what anyone might say.

Dented tins are always vastly reduced. They are fine if the tin isn't actually punctured or 'blown'. Don't eat if the contents are the least bit off. In hundreds of dented tins I've only ever found one we couldn't eat.

Rusks can be made at home, never bought in a chemist's packet. Cut up leftover bread/cake/sandwiches and put them on a baking tray in the oven after you've removed whatever was cooking. There'll be enough heat left to dry them out and crisp them.

Cakes from the day before are half-price or less the next day. Some bakeries display these; others don't. If you're new to poverty you can hide any shame by requesting 'stale cake for a trifle'. Out-of-date cakes of the packaged sort are sometimes given away by nice shopkeepers.

Bruised bananas, even if almost black outside, are usually delicious within. Snap them up whenever they're offered. They are better than sound ones for banana custards and other nursery puddings. If you're offered bruised apples or pears, however, decline gracefully without spoiling your chances for the bananas next time (or say yes and take them home for the chickens).

Perhaps the most important rule about shopping for food is to be always cheerful and pleasant without obliterating the fact that you aren't a millionaire. If you're not in an exclusively supermarket belt get in with obliging small shopkeepers and stay with them. You're doing them a favour and they'll look after you.

Should you buy the child a packet of dolly-mixtures every day and order half a pint of double cream for Sundays, then nobody's going to think of you when the out-of-date battenburgs come up. I'm now in receipt of an irregular supply of very small but altogether sound potatoes absolutely free. These unsaleables used to go to an old man for his pigs. Said the shopkeeper, '... I wondered what on earth I was doing. He has half an ounce of tobacco every single day ... he can't be exactly hard up. So ... if you wouldn't be offended ...'

Children are good at winning the hearts of susceptible tradesmen though there are broad conditions of behaviour. Whining, meddling with displays and asking for things is out. Generous tradespeople like good children who don't expect treats. Train your little ambassadors.

Large packets of commodities are usually cheaper weight-for-weight than are the smaller-sized, but this isn't invariably so. If you're passable at maths try to work it out before you go for bulk bargains. Washing-up liquid is famous for confusing the innumerate: the first 'bulk' size (two litres, say) can often be more expensive than buying X number of squeezy bottles to the same measure. Buy the *next* size up, though, and you've got a bargain. Very big bulk (for instance six months' supply) of anything is always cheaper. Finding the cash outlay is the problem. You can make big, big savings on jumbo cornflour, custard powder, pasta (dry), soya 'meat', dried milk, oatmeal, cornflakes. But try to keep your really enormous bulks deadly boring, otherwise, if you're like us, you'll gorge. Once I bought a gallon of tomato sauce, in a catering pot like a goldfish bowl, sure that it would last for months, and all food was thereafter scarlet until, within three weeks, the stuff was gone. We had a similar slip-up over chocolate bars: I bought a boxful to last for ever as the goody in my working son's daily lunch pack. Four days, I think, was the record there! On the other hand a kilo or two of, say, Bisto, is quite safe.

Remember that *flour* doesn't keep all that long. Inevitably it catches weevils and you find the stuff full of little cobwebs. Each autumn I buy a couple of huge sacks from the bakery simply because, living over fields as we do, every parcel and basket must be heaved across by hand; so I take advantage of anyone willing to risk their exhaust pipes to deliver a sale worth delivering. By spring it's generally weevily, but seems to cook all right.

Free food can be absolute, as with Luncheon Vouchers, meals with work (domestic, canteen, hotel, or pub), free school dinners and free milk, or it can be of the wild kind; the growing in the hedgerow type. Even if you live in the most crowded part of the city you can take a bus out as far as the first blackberry bushes. Puddings, jams, jellies or just blackberries on their own are as dependable as Christmas. It is always a good year for blackberries. From the end of August to the first of October, when the fairies are said to spit on them.

Never stir from home without a plastic carrier bag. You never know what you'll find. Mushrooms and toadstools are fine for those of us who dare, but you'd be surprised how many people won't contemplate fungi that haven't come from a shop. Our family gathers – among almost anything else that extrudes from damp earth or tree stump – 'inkpots'. Inkpots are slippery, are milder than field mushrooms and insist upon being eaten young. Should you wait too long before you gather them your carrier bag could literally be awash before you get home.

It's essential to own identification handbooks on both fungi and wild plants and fruits, preferably those which also tell you how to prepare and cook your finds.

Among the things you might consider getting used to are young nettles (boiled as 'spinach' or as soup), dandelion leaves, fat hen (like spinach – again), elderberries (for jam, jelly, wine, dried as currants), hawthorn shoots – sometimes called 'bread and cheese' (used in salads, added to mashed potato, mixed into dumplings, in Marmite sandwiches). The list could be almost endless, wild pears and apples, sloes for jelly or gin, watercress, chickweed (spinach for the third time!). I've even been served up ground elder, boiled like cabbage. It was not very nice.

One could go on more about ferreting a living, scrounging and scraping. The thing is that, with never enough money, the life instinct of hunting-saving-making-do does tend to become the be-all-end-all of general budgeting. Often it has to be. So, here in the middle of a chapter on existing cheaply, is probably the best place to site a little encouragement – no more – to country single-parents who might be on the brink of what's generally known as The Self-Sufficient Life. Volumes have already been done on keeping hens, goats, bees, cows; on making cheese, yogurt, cottage pâté; on growing turnips, peas, vegetable marrows. Let me add, as a thoroughly convinced self-supplier, that it works. Legs of roasted kid, cream cheeses swinging away in little muslin cloths, muscovy duck à l'orange, swedes in a clamp, plums in kilner jars, apples wrapped against winter, bunches of herbs stuck behind the clock: it's the most extraordinarily rich existence for hapless one-parents.

Books to read if you're this way inclined (and I wasn't initially but it can really grow on you) are the Hindes' On Next to

Nothing and the Seymours' *Self-Sufficiency*. An extra delight if you can spare the cash is Dorothy Hartley's *Food in England*: here's the history, growing and cooking of food which knocks Mrs Beeton into a cook's hat. Mrs Hartley even tells you how to construct your own bread oven, cheese press, or privy.

I'm aware of becoming a bore about it, and I won't mention it again after this, but I do wish more one-parents would consider turning their heads towards the bounty of nature.

Sundry furnishings or the feathering of our nest is essential to comfort, warmth, and decency. You may find a bed with passable mattress for £2, an armchair for 60p, a gas cooker in moderate nick for under a fiver: *auctions* are the thing for the new Linear Family without much money to set up house. If you're new to the salerooms (or, better, the auction *in situ*) take a friend with you. It's curious how difficult it is to pluck up courage enough to bid for the first time. With two it's fun. Don't take children unless they're particularly passive. A twitching anxious mother could well find herself inadvertently putting in a bid for a Boulle commode.

Oxfam is good for bedding, curtains, china and glass, plastic and tin, baby equipment. It is unusual, though not impossible, to find knock-down furniture or very large items there, and some branches are cheaper than others, but most are emenable to offers if you can't afford what they're asking.

Social Services always have a stock of free baby bedding and can often supply free prams, cots, playpens and so on. Just be bold enough to make contact when you're on your uppers. You don't have to be a 'case' in order to be eligible for hand-outs.

The Women's Royal Voluntary Service supply all sorts of furniture and household equipment, carpets and bedding. They only oblige on the recommendation of Social Services, Gingerbread and the like as it's the only way they can ensure their stuff goes to the really needy. Otherwise everyone would roll up to collect a free Hoovermatic or stair-carpet. All goods are second-hand, so what exactly is in store at any one time depends absolutely upon current generosity.

Clinics, surgeries, even launderettes, sometimes have a notice board where anyone can pin up 'For Sale' notices or beg 'Wants'. This is a fruitful way of attracting furniture, bicycles, baby gear. Newsagents make a minute charge for a similar service.

Jumble and rummage sales are great for odd pieces of crockery and kitchen utensils, but avoid defunct electrical goods which tend to end their days at such a junket. Get there in good time if you want early pickings of the hardware and household: get there towards the end if you're after *clothing* because jumbles are mostly clothes, and the organizers don't want to be left with a monumental heap of unsold garments. My second overcoat (not the WRVS one, which has fur inside) cost two pence at a PTA sale, and many a boy's jersey I've bought for a penny. Pairs of socks are practically given away – an armful for five pence. Adults' cotton dresses can be snapped up for a penny, taken home and turned into pillow-cases or tea towels. Old ladies' tweed skirts of fantastic quality, with all-silk linings and the Woolmark (there are always masses of these, I suspect from the effects of deceased great-grandmas) can be transformed into little boys' winter trousers or little girls' pinafore frocks, into patchwork blankets (large squares feather-stitched together, double-sided) or pram rugs.

As the years of one-parenting gather up behind me so has my knowledge of local jumble sales accordingly increased. My politics function only in relation to autumn fund-raising sales. I know exactly which ones to attend for the second-hand Chilprufe, the all-wool (cashmere even) sweaters, the silver lamé for the dressing-up box. I found full Masonic regalia at one, not to mention Newmarket boots and an Eton Rambler's tie.

Children's clothes can also be obtained from the Social Services and all types of garments (on recommendation) from WRVS.

Good-as-new shops have become chic. They are as far removed from the old image of the Second-Hand Clothes Shop as is my idea of a dress allowance from that of Her Majesty. I can, with judicious choosing, spend 10p at a jumble sale on a garment which, good-as-new, would knock me back (albeit washed and ironed) three or four pounds. These shops are useful, however, for school uniforms ... which are unbelievably expensive to buy new.

Many schools which insist upon uniform being worn run a second-hand scheme. Ask the secretary. Still, remember that no primary school can compel any child to wear uniform. None of mine did.

Feet are not as amenable to second-hands as are other areas of the human form. Second-hand shoes really can cause deformed toes, bumpy joints, gross discomfort. New ones, measured up for length and width, are so expensive one can only swoon and pray for miracles; so if you really can't afford new ones, then be bold enough to contact the DHSS and ask for a special grant. Even if you're not drawing SB it's worth putting your case. The Social Services could back you up. All this takes time – weeks perhaps – during which period of investigation the DHSS doubtless imagine your barefoot child happy to wait. Buy him new plimsolls rather than second-hand shoes, but keep pressing for a decision. Second-hand wellingtons are all right, one size too big, worn with a couple of pairs of socks.

If your child is of school age you'll be eligible for a periodic clothing allowance from the County Education Authority. All low-income families (and all, automatically, on SB) are free to claim. Most children are sent home at the end of summer term with a potential application form in respect of clothing/meals/maintenance for over-sixteens. If you don't receive such a form, or if you're taken rather more than short between official applications, get in touch with the school secretary or write direct to your area Education Office.

Energy This includes electricity, gas, coal, paraffin, and petrol. I'd imagine that few enough single-parents are directly worried by the cost of petrol. It's the bill for heating our houses and cooking our meals that triggers off the recurring trauma. Many of us spend up to a third of our weekly income on 'energy'. Little meannesses are imperative. Most are obvious, though unheeded in more moneyed circles.

Learn to switch off behind you, and teach the children likewise.

Use low-watt bulbs in passages, halls, any place where close scrutiny is least important, which does not include stairs. Sometimes I remove bulbs altogether during summer months.

Lag the hot-water cylinder with an eiderdown, sleeping-bag, old overcoats or blankets if a proper 'jacket' is beyond you. Use the top of the hot tank for airing clothes, bedding and drying tights.

Start being stingy about bath water: two people or more can use the same. Rinse out pants, tights, school socks in redundant bath water. If you have a working teenager who expects you to wash oily boiler suits, add detergent to second-hand water and soak those abominations clean overnight.

Don't fill the kettle fuller than you need. Save any boiling water in a thermos flask for next cup of coffee. Or wash-up with it, make a jelly, scald out the sink down-pipe.

Always cook as much as you can in a single pot. An enormous saucepan, crammed full and tightly lidded, will use no more electricity on lowest heat than will a small pan, half empty and lidless.

Ditto the oven. If you must cook one dish, then cook two or three more at the same time for the same cost. You also get the bonus of having saved on tomorrow's chores.

Remember that the most economically crippling appliances are any electric fires you may use (switch off a bar) and an immersion heater. Cut down with cunning over a single quarter and assess the difference.

An open fire (supposing you don't live in a smoke-free zone) can be a tremendous saver, especially so if you burn wood. One Cambridge lone parent heats her house entirely by gathering discarded doors, sills and skirting boards from building sites (the demolition bit of such sites, obviously). She's also gathered a charming iron bedstead and an incredible steel butterfly fire-guard for which any collectors of thirties memorabilia would give his soul.

Dead wood lies about beside public footpaths: gather it up. The same goes for branches and so on that lie on common ground. You need no sanction. For the building site, need one say, you must ask the foreman before you glean. Usually he will fall over himself to be helpful. Quite apart from it being nice for him to have a woman around, his men are saved the trouble of making a bonfire of demolished rubbish.

Should you seriously decide to join the wood-burners some basic tools are essential. Two, in fact. A bowsaw and a small axe. If, like my Cambridge friend, you depend upon dismantled builders' waste, a good sledgehammer is a useful addition to the armoury. There's something compulsive about the hewing of wood and even quite small children can help with the lighter pieces.

An old-fashioned trivet (from a junk shop or tame black-smith) or even a spare house brick will hold a saucepan or kettle against an open fire. Boil/stew as much as you can 'against the fire'. Don't forget the heap of ever-hot ash below the fire either. Wrap potatoes in foil and push them into it for marvellous baked spuds.

Warning: it is illegal to burn an unguarded fire where there are children in the house. A nursery-type guard isn't cheap, but is one of the items you may have to spend your money on.

Paraffin heaters are the cheapest means of keeping a room warm. They are also potentially lethal if improperly used, im-properly guarded or if left in a room with unattended children – even for five minutes. Never leave an oil-stove burning in a child's bedroom overnight. Nor in your own room, come to that. Don't try to cook on top of a paraffin heater which is designed for 'domestic warmth' only. There are single-burner cookers which are designed for the job.

When your economies are reaching desperation pitch you may cook by even less conventional means. Rice, if brought up to the boil for two or three minutes, can be taken from the stove, the pan lid clamped on tightly and the whole thing thoroughly wrapped up in an old blanket. Carry this extra-ordinary burden upstairs and pop it down your bed. Tuck the bedclothes snugly round it, take the children to school and yourself to work, and forget about the stranger in your bed until you return at tea time. The rice will then be cooked, still hot, and all ready to eat!

A wide-topped thermos flask will cook for free too. If you put raw rice, boiling milk, and sugar all together in the flask, screw down the top and go away, you will have rice pudding when you return, some soups, such as vegetable and chicken noodle, can be cooked like this too. The thing to remember is not to try anything that will need stirring to prevent lumps, so anything flour-based is out.

This list could go on into the night, an endless catalogue of corners to cut, pounds to save, meals to produce from supple-mented H_2O. You can smoke tea-leaves or dried banana skins, you can wear two pairs of tights at once, trusting in the law of averages to arrange the holes above or below a sound area, you can sleep with the dusk and rise with the dawn when the electricity worries you, you can hang the wet nappies straight out on the line in a thunder storm, you can ... you can ...

Parsimony continually stretches the mind, becomes, in a way, pretty liberating, and how the highlights, when they do come, are magnified!

Further reading

On Next to Nothing, by Susan and Thomas Hinde (Sphere 1977)

Complete Book of Self-Sufficiency, by John Seymour (Faber 1976)

Food in England, by Dorothy Hartley (Macdonald 1975)

all from the library

See Appendix

Buy Bulk Bureau

Women's Royal Voluntary Service

14 Letting the child go

'When they're off my hands ... ten years hence, fifteen at the most ... what then? Will I be too old to have a life of my own?' So writes one mother who, for years past, has known nothing beyond her children and their needs. She has seen herself only as an offshoot of Cubs and Brownies, school plays and rummage sales, birthday outings and quarantine for measles. Her fighting maternal instincts filled her life, until a small and subtle warning light appeared at the end of the Linear tunnel. 'Family', in this tight and sufficient wholeness, is a phase of built-in obsolescence in which the progression of time itself determines our redundancy as a physical parent.

It's difficult, when we're still deep in the comfortable chaos of rearing those children, to see out far enough into that inescapable gap which stretches between their growing up and our growing old. And that gap exists for all of us as surely as their inexorable journey towards adulthood.

We ought meanwhile not only to glimpse the children's future, but also our own. I mean that, buried all along with our one-parenting, we would do well to keep warm any latent personal plans, ready to put into practice when the children leave home. We cannot make a career out of motherhood and then petulantly refuse to take our retirement.

Even in the best-run Triangular Families one finds – frequently – that the youngest child remains a 'baby' far in excess of his siblings at a similar age. There is no hurry for him to mature as nobody else is toddling along eighteen months behind him. This babying is also, in part, a subconscious effort on behalf of the mother to keep herself young through administering to a little child. The single parent is also open to such temptations only more so. The child is too often all she's got and her natural instinct is to hang on.

Not infrequently this intensity of care induces a sense of mutual dependence. Neither parent nor child can function without the complementary other half. It is a mere whisker's breadth away from romantic love: both people are emotionally blocked up. He/she cannot move from the mother into a normal girl/boy relationship. She cannot move from him or her into a life of her own. Both are caught in an unadventurous and self-satisfied situation which can so easily become the end-all of their story if neither takes on the job of breaking the *status quo*.

Men who have been brought up like precious jewels, their socks ironed and their toast de-crusted, may react in one of two opposite ways – they could bolt from the smothering motherliness as soon as they save the fare to do so, or settle for being spoilt. Homosexuality or celibacy are more likely.

Children are instinctively solicitous, and somehow we have to get through to them at a fairly early age that we can look after ourselves when we have to. I don't mean that we should set about blunting their sensibilities nor making them feel that we are trying to reject them: we mustn't rudely push them away when they express concern. Neither must we play upon their infant anxiety.

Andrew, for instance, starting school at four-and-a-half, was worried that I'd be lonely while he was away. 'Will you be all right?' he used to ask, 'All right without me?' It sounded so sweet, and it would have been easy to make a meal out of the situation, playing it out with protestations of my desolation at his absence. His natural concern would only have been doubled, worsened. So I made a point of telling him about all the things I'd been up to while he was at school. He could then build up a picture of me feeding the hens, peeling the potatoes, typing the pages, and thus seeing that I wasn't actually sitting about mooning for his return. Get out of the child what he's been up to all day too, so that a pattern of independence between breakfast and tea is early taken for granted. He will learn that we must have part of each day 'on our own'.

Some children, nearing the age of independence, are suddenly struck with guilt when planning to leave home. Are they 'abandoning' mother who, when they are gone, will inherit (they reckon) a purposeless life? This is, of course, sheer adolescent arrogance, though they don't see it that way and would be bitterly hurt to hear it.

Make sure they understand that you have other interests beyond the home and family (even if it means taking up some seemingly absorbing hobby *pro tem*) and that they understand that you don't expect their devotion in the form of physical presence. And never suggest their reluctance to go might be bound up with gratitude. No child must ever be made to feel grateful for having been reared.

The less extrovert one-parent child may almost incidentally opt to remain at home, not through anything as complex as guilt or gratitude, but purely because he is too comfortable to make any spontaneous move.

Of course there never actually comes a day when you have to say, 'Out! I've done enough for you!' The time does come, though, when you must begin to help a child into the wider world. Resurrect contacts away from home: negotiate for a training course or work experience at some distance, and angle for digs. Put the germs of plans into his mind and be around to do the encouraging when action gets slack. Once away the child will mature, will find the world – with luck – agreeable. And, after all, he's at liberty to come home as much as he pleases and this may be an awful lot at first.

Some older children are drawn back to the 'absent' parent after they start work and plan their own freedom. You can't stop them and you ought to have ceased worrying by now, anyway.

When they are truly gone you must honour their independence and enjoy it with them. Take an interest in their training, jobs and families, but don't dare interfere, and never offer advice unless it's asked for. See they understand, however, that you are always there – and that your door is always open to them – should trouble ever descend. Don't be like the (admittedly elderly) mother who, when her distraught daughter telephoned to ask if she could bring her two children back to the family home until her own marriage problems were sorted out, said that the spare room needed decorating and could they make it later on in the summer?

15 In care:
a brief explanation

Sixty per cent of the 100,600 children 'in care' are one-parented: many are in residential Homes, others are settled into private families as 'foster children'. About a third of fostered children stay with relatives or friends who are entitled to the relevant boarding-out allowances. Yet, ironically, we as natural parents cannot double as our own foster-parents, even though that allowance might make all the difference between being able to cope and floundering hopelessly. It's tempting to indulge in a trough of low spirits when one compares the 'ordinary' (i.e. non-specialist) fostering maintenance paid by local authorities to the sum deemed sufficient by the DHSS when we draw Supplementary Benefit. Most foster parents draw up to four times the maintenance that natural parents receive (per child) on SB, yet that child's needs are no different, materially, whichever woman feeds and clothes him.

Now Granny – who, say, lives next door to you – may be approved as foster mother (so long as the child is received into care under *Section 1*, see below) and as such will be eligible for support from council funds. Yet should you, the working mother, elect to move in with Granny for economical, social or plain good-sense reasons, then she will no longer be regarded as a *bona fide* foster mother. Financial support will be withdrawn. The baby could be moved on.

The child in care is, to a great extent, a pawn in a game with complex and overlapping rules. Your part is to prevent the special child in your life from joining those 50,000-plus children who have exchanged, on the practical level, one parent for no parent. Even so, be prepared for pressing and unavoidable events: we cannot all be immune to the meaner acts of God.

Ill-health in the single parent is probably the main reason behind our children being taken into care. This is closely followed by the second reason: that state of chronic panic which spawns an inability to cope with job/finances/family to the point of hopelessness. Other and sadder one-parents forsake their children, in one motion or by degrees.

Supposing, then, you have no alternative and must ask that your child be received into care, albeit temporarily, what are the terms? He is at this stage received into care under *Section 1* of the *Children's Act 1948*. He may be fostered for a period of up to six months with any one family, during which time you are at liberty to take him out of care without undue preamble as soon as your own particular problems are solved. After this six months' limit you are required by law to give twenty-eight days' notice of your intention to have him back to live with you unless the local authority agrees you should have him sooner. This leeway is sensible and allows time for the child to prepare for home-going which is especially important if he has been away for some time without contact – if, for instance, you have been in hospital. Young children forget very quickly.

If, after a minimum of three years in care, there is still no foreseeable prospect of reunion, the local authority is free to consider the next step – the assumption of *Parental Rights*, which means that both in law and in practice they accept the role of parenthood. This is usually in concern for the child's security and long-term plans for his future. The parent may not always be consulted, though she will be informed of any changes made. She does have the right of appeal to a Juvenile Court, but this must be registered within twenty-eight days of the order. There are all sorts of reasons why a local authority may take parental rights over a child, but it is only recently (1975) that the mere passage of time gives them the right to do so.

If your circumstances change for the better after parental rights have been vested in the local authority the order can be rescinded, so long as all parties are certain that such a reversal is in the best interests of the child.

When any child has been with the same foster parents for a minimum of five years, then those foster parents are at liberty to apply for an *Adoption Order* without the permission of either natural parents or the local authority. Obviously you can oppose this, though you're not going to look too rosy in the eyes of the judiciary if you've only made spasmodic visits throughout the child's separation from you.

It is, for many reasons beyond humanitarian caring, vital to keep in touch once the child is with foster parents. Even if he is away for a comparatively short while (perhaps while you're having another baby) don't neglect the postcards or the telephone calls. Ask a friend or relative who really knows the child well, and whom the child likes, to stand in for you when personal visiting isn't possible. Once you appear to have lost interest the long-term views may not be easy to assess. It is the facts that count.

Social Services are empowered to hand out free travel warrants (British Rail) if fairly heavy costs are involved in making visits. Ask for these if you're short of cash.

Every six months each child's 'case' is reviewed. The present progress and future prospects of rehabilitation and/or long-term care are discussed, any changes thought politic are approved, and the child's life is 'planned' for the following half-year. Foster parents ask to be included in 'case reviews' (some authorities automatically extend an invitation). Parents might also ask to be present: there is nothing in law to obstruct your attendance at this gathering which is discussing your own child's immediate future. Never be afraid of making a nuisance of yourself when you feel constructive about a given predicament. But don't just bawl for bawling's sake.

Other than reception into care under *Section 1*, children may find themselves in a similar predicament following a court ruling. This is usually through the Juvenile Court, but a Matrimonial Court may also place a child in the care of the local authority. In law this is known as a *Care Order*.

If any situation is so acute that immediate action is imperative, then a *Place of Safety Order* is taken out and this secures a child's removal from home forthwith. That case must then necessarily come up before the Juvenile Court, where evidence will be heard and decisions made upon actions to be taken. The Social Services, the police and the NSPCC all hold power to serve such orders. Never give them a chance to do so. Never give the neighbours, either, a chance to put in any complaint.

If the worst happens, be sure you are always legally represented; and never go to any court hearing without the support of a good friend or neighbour. It is so easy to be emotionally squashed when met by the convolutions of British law: experiences can be humiliating and embittering. Be tough.

Whatever the outcome, always remember that circumstances change; and when yours change for the better any decisions made can be reversed. Only legal adoption can take your child away from you for ever, (and even then, at eighteen, any person may ask to see his original birth certificate, it's then up to him to burrow back into his past or not, as he feels).

Parents looking for temporary foster care may deliberately use private sources. Many private foster parents are excellent, but others have been turned down as unsuitable for local authority placements. Although registered, these homes may only meet minimum standards. Regular visits are made by area social workers, who are entitled to contact parents independently should any real doubts arise.

The single parent who is afraid that her child, if placed voluntarily in care, will become too enmeshed in the vagaries of the Social Services, may choose to foster privately. The selection of a given home is hers alone and removal from that home is simplicity itself compared with the ramifications of The Welfare. Independent fostering, intelligently used, can suit us on occasion.

Social workers should, in advance of placing a child with foster parents, give the natural mother an idea of the type of family to be used. The mother's opinion will be heeded. She is also entitled to request removal of her child from a home she does not approve (though removal isn't guaranteed). Some mothers may actually prefer their children to be in the less rivalling atmosphere of a residential Home. If you feel this way, say so.

All welfare workers are human and as such inevitably differ one from the other. Some are more reasonable than others in considering parents' idiosyncrasies.

Fostering in some areas is both easily forthcoming and of a high standard. In others it's inevitably full up and in less than first-class order. There's an awful lot of luck in geography.

Above all, put your feelers out before making any move: never tackle a block-busting problem without the sympathetic advice of a professional helper or a companion of deep understanding: and always bear in mind – and see that nobody else forgets the fact – that the child concerned is yours.

See Appendix

Apart-Aid

Association of British Fostering and Adoption Agencies

Church of England Children's Society

CAB

Dr Barnardo's

Family Rights Group

Gingerbread

National Council for One Parent Families

National Children's Home

National Foster Care Association

Thomas Coram Foundation

16 Getting out of the one-parent family

Failure in one marriage doesn't necessarily immunize us against another attack. On the contrary the majority of people faced with single-parenthood during their early twenties – or before – do remarry. However, the later you fall into the Linear the less marketable you're likely to be. Real determination must be mobilized if you're resolute about returning to the Triangular.

Anybody, male or female, plain or passable, ought to be able to find a mate if they really make a career of it. For some it is as essential as life's blood, particularly for those who, after working hard at being a single parent and finding it satisfactory in the broadest sense, still feel lonely within themselves. The picture of happy, well-adjusted, secure children need not imply (though true, it usually does) that the parent's emotions are also placated. However self-reliant we may be, there are times when most of us miss the presence of a partner, not specifically miss our old partner, but miss having any adult at all to share, on a simple level, the pleasures of bringing up the family.

Some parents never do manage to fend off the crippling isolation and really the only let-out for them is a new and permanent relationship. They cannot function as 'whole' without having some male adult at home with them. This emotional vacuum has nothing to do with the depth of affection felt for the children. We concede that the children are loved a lot, but this unilateral love might not be enough.

The common deterrent to marriage or remarriage rests with our practical desolation. The greater number of us are out of the very young, very attractive range, and ties of home and children are just about as tightly knotted as they can be. We tend to be overlooked on social occasions where 'couples' are the vogue. As paupers unable to afford baby-sitters we seldom go out for child-unrelated pleasure. Some find that friends, happily married to each other, become apprehensive about inviting us to their homes because of our threatening single status. Our freedom, to them, is a sexual threat while, to us, it becomes a barrier to social exchange. On paper, it would seem that in addition to our famous Poverty Trap we also must carry a Catch-22 Status Trap. One-parents who are rendered claustrophobic by this theory ought to lay their plans for escape before getting bogged down in what can only be, for them, an emotionally problematic future.

First, clearly understand that no golden prince is coming to seek you out: the chances are that nobody outside your immediate circle knows you exist. It is you who must emerge, and you'll find ways if you really want to. What about starting off on the good old standby of evening classes? And stop turning down invitations. Remember, partners are met in the most unlikely places so look about and be pleasant to everyone, for who knows where it will lead? One of my friends, saddled for years with two demanding children, met a fiercely red-bearded man at a Youth Hostel while on a hiking holiday with her little gaolers. This ham-fisted gentleman, struggling and practically slashing his wrists while opening a tin of soup in the hostel kitchen, was rescued by stout, greying, efficient B and her noisy girls. As it turned out, permanently rescued. And she wasn't even consciously hoping.

If, in spite of your forays into the world, no possible mate so much as dents the horizon, then formal action is another option: the marriage bureaux, friendship clubs, dating agencies. In this country, where arranged marriages are hardly *de rigueur*, it takes a certain amount of courage even to approach such an institution. This obstacle which results from guilt/fear of failure/ fear of ridicule, is incredibly hard to circumnavigate. Still, for the single-parent at her last ditch there's little choice if she's quite resolved to share her declining years with a nice old man. She must take the plunge or settle bitterly in with her loneliness. She has, in effect, to advertise herself as vacant and as open to offers.

As *Dateline* puts it: 'It's sad to feel that people have to write to us to arrange meetings, but that's what we're here for and we try our hardest to make them feel that somewhere someone is right for them ... once you assure a person of this fact it's surprising how quickly barriers are broken and they start really to try ... no matter what skeletons are hiding in the cupboard!'

The skeleton, in our case, is the 'drawback' of children, the existence of which *Dateline* (and probably others) imagine is a great putter-off if divulged during initial steps. '... this [deception] gives an applicant a chance to present herself *as* herself without attaching a label, e.g. "three kids" ... from the word go. There is a real problem of being single with children.'

So, you meet the man, hit it off, then bring out the surprise snapshots of the family on last year's holiday, do you? Let's hope that he has a secret brood too!

No doubt these experienced matchmakers know what they're up to, but personally I feel that any cover-up concerning such important appendages as our children is vastly improper. Are we meant to be ashamed of our plurality? To say, 'He's marrying you, not the children,' is simply not true. He's marrying the lot of you.

I suggest using an agency where children are counted in as a vital section of the deal. Unfortunately there exists no central association to which agencies must subscribe, there are no 'approved' bureaux as such, no scale of set fees or code of practice. Literally anybody may start up a marriage bureau and run it exactly as they please: so how does the uninitiated seeker choose?

The best bet is to go for the long-established ones, the ones you see advertised in 'reputable' publications; and don't be hurried into adding your name to their lists. Either telephone or make a personal visit. Don't, initially, make contact by letter, as it's so much easier to get the feel of a service and judge the sincerity of the people who run it on a voice-to-voice level. Ask all the questions you want to ask, particularly their attitude towards children, before you decide to use any bureau. Ask, too, about annual fees. These generally range from between £25 to £45 depending upon age and accessibility: an amiable middle-aged mother living in a remote Cumbrian village would, most likely, get a longer time-limit than a paradisical beauty with one child living on the outskirts of London. The more work for the agency, the higher the fee: thus the younger and minimally encumbered pay less (usually) than the choosy, plain or regularly prolific. But when it comes down to reality it's all in the luck of the draw.

However, if you truly can't bring yourself to subscribe to the bureau trade, and if your roots are not deep nor your larger possessions many, don't forget the housekeeping field of search.

Not infallible, all right. But a strong possibility (see page 41).

The best times for remarriage, from the point of view of causing the least family disruption, are when the children are still babies or when they are ready, themselves, to leave home. We already know of the hostility often felt by children above the age of reason; though small children, those below five or six years old, generally prey upon attentive men, for their cunning is deep. Men wanting to 'please' mother will frequently 'spoil' her children.

One thirteen-year-old, on inquiry, felt it to be the duty of her mother to talk the matter of possible marriage over within the family first. If the children felt they didn't like the man – and couldn't ever come to like the man – then the idea of marriage must be dropped. This girl's opinion was that she herself would feel 'put out', 'left out' and even 'deserted'. If some sort of partnership were inevitable, then this same girl would prefer a 'living together' rather than marriage. 'You get a chance then to see if you can learn to co-exist with him ... perhaps even learn to love him,' she says. On the other hand she would expect him to consider the children equally with his new wife. If he is rich (and certainly the family is going to be better off thanks to his joining them), then the older children expect to be consulted about certain changes in life style. 'I mean, we might not want all that carpeting or a drinks bar or whatever he plans to install,' says a fourteen-year-old boy. 'We children might be contented with the house as it always has been.' The idea of actually moving house with the new marriage struck these two as unthinkable: 'But we're happy as we are,' they wailed.

This, I imagine, is the crux of the matter. If the single-parent has really created a happy family atmosphere – and we all know by now that this is very probable – then it's likely that the children will oppose interference or change. The man (any man) may be regarded as enemy.

'What if we can't take to him, however we try?' asks a nine-year-old boy. What indeed? This same child imagined that his older brother, who had during the years since their father's death been honorary head of the family, would feel jealous. And that's quite a point to think about too.

A sixteen-year-old said he wouldn't mind his mother marrying again now, though he would have hated it when he was younger. 'But I can't see the others [his younger sisters] thinking much of it.' The chances are, then, that criticism will come thick and fast. Your man may not be their style. Be ready for quite sophisticated ridicule but don't get in a huff about it. Try, if you're not too decrepit, to home in on their level and give as good as you get, yet without dismissing their opinions altogether. I don't believe any children have a right to force the direction of their parents' private lives, but remember that they think otherwise. Tread carefully and diplomatically: their observations may be clearer than yours.

Everybody's different. All single parents. All one-parented children. Nobody thinks or wants in an exactly predictable manner. All I can do is have a look at a good sample and conclude what most parents and what most children seem to think about remarriage.

A great many parents, particularly those whose marriages have been really rotten, don't want to remarry, though comparatively few are so put off that they opt for total celibacy. A small proportion, though not so small as to merit silence, turn right around and become homosexual. Present-day children being brought up within openly homosexual families are among the first generation to experience, without pretence, two parents of the same sex. This may well be hard for them, especially during the adolescent years when tolerance and understanding of grown-ups is at its lowest. There is an association for lesbian mothers which offers advice on parenting, helps with personal and legal problems and acts as a social spring-board for mothers, their partners and their children (see Appendix).

The majority of single mothers would like, ideally, some sort of new relationship with the opposite sex, though not necessarily marriage. This relationship may be secondary to the role of mothering. Lone fathers I've talked to seem keener on a regularized union, with what they imagine would constitute 'security' for their children.

Remarriage of the absent parent doesn't present such a plethora of consequences. A lot of single-parents and their children seem actively relieved when their erstwhile spouse/father or mother remarries, foreseeing less interference and hassle with their 'ex' safely interested elsewhere.

Some adolescent children, particularly girls, are happy for the absent parent to remarry because they feel for his/her loneliness – real or imagined. Other children who, even sub-consciously, never cease to hope their mother and father will 'make it up', see the absent parent's remarriage as the final barrier to this desired end. Such children may go through a 'difficult' phase after the remarriage, and much understanding – by all parties, if possible – will be called for.

And for those who do start again in the Triangular structure you may be interested to learn that the general consensus among a group of teenagers may be typified thus: 'I feel at ease with my new "step" but don't come anywhere near loving him. I'm able to accept my little half-brother with love, but not his father . . . not entirely.'

Appendix

Aaron Silverman Trust, 35 Parliament Hill, Hampstead, London NW3 2TA, 01-435 5831. Will meet costs of medical, welfare and social services in cases of need. Also: *Apart-Aid*, same address, which provides a counselling and legal service. Aims to fill the gap between individual self-help and any statutory assistance the Social Services are able to provide. No charge. Offices in Farnborough (Hants), Wakefield (Yorks), Reading (Berks), Ipswich (Suffolk), Mansfield (Notts), Portsmouth (Hants) and Leicester.

Action for Lesbian Parents, 57 Maid's Causeway, Cambridge, CB5 8DE, Cambridge 66841. Particularly anxious to help mothers in custody/access cases. General help and advice. Friendly and uncensorious.

Anatomist General (DHSS), Alexander Fleming House, Elephant and Castle, London SE1 6BY. Apropos making arrangements in the event of the immediately unlikely. The above address for relevant forms and information on bequeathing your body for medical research.

Association of British Adoption and Fostering Agencies, 4 Southampton Row, London WC1B 4AA, 01-242 8951. For advice, counselling and referrals.

Association of Widows in Great Britain, 56 Gainsborough Road, Grindon, Sunderland, Hylton 2256. Campaigns for changes in taxation laws.

British Tourist Authority, 64 St James's Street, London SW1A 1NF, 01-629 9191. For getting your bed-and-breakfast/paying guests accommodation listed in the relevant guides.

Buttle Trust, Audley House, 300 Vauxhall Bridge Road, London SW1V 1AJ, 01-828 7311. Will consider the making of grants to various categories of children, with strong slant towards helping the single-parented child. Maintenance, special needs and clothing, school fees in exceptional circumstances. Members of the Christian faith (any denomination).

Buy Bulk Bureau, 18 Queen Anne's Gate, London SW1H 9AA, 01-839 2846. Cheaper living through pooling orders and sharing out. Useful for groups of single parents.

Children's Country Holidays Fund, 1 York Street, London W1, 01-935 8373. Many, many single-parented children enjoy a greatly subsidized holiday each summer. Billeted on private families (all thoroughly vetted). Farms are favourite.

Child Guidance Clinics (local telephone book) for help with children's behaviour problems, educational blocks and social regressions. On recommendation of doctor, school head, or make contact yourself.

Child Poverty Action Group, 1 Maklin Street, London WC2 5NH, 01-242 3225. Pressure group dedicated to fair financial benefits for all children. Queries answered. Around sixty local groups already functioning. Help with tribunal representation.

Church of England Children's Society, Old Town Hall, Kennington Road, London SE11 4QD, 01-735 2441. Day-care in centres countrywide for under-fives. Latch Key Clubs for after-school care. Play schemes for school holidays. Family case work. Special centres include provision for short holidays for parents under stress. Limited housing schemes for one-parent families in West Country.

Citizens' Advice Bureau, 26 Bedford Square, London WC1. In case you can't locate any of the 100 or so nationwide offices (or one of the visiting vans) contact headquarters. Advice and sympathetic help on all problems. Never any charge for counselling.

Citizens' Rights Office, 1 Maklin Street, London WC2 5NH, 01-405 5942. Advice on Social Security and Supplementary Benefits queries only. Office open 1.30 to 5.30 p.m. weekdays. Appointments only.

Corrections Department, Office of Population, Censuses and Surveys, St Catherine's House, Kingsway, London WC2B 6JP, 01-242 0262. Will advise on problems connected with birth certificates.

Council for Voluntary Service, 96 High Street West, Tyne and Wear NE28 8HY. Acts as springboard for one-parent groups in Tyneside and environs. Social, self-help, advice. One of the first organizations to push the 'Grannies for single-parent families' idea.

Cruse, 126 Sheen Road, Richmond, Surrey TW9 1UR, 01-940 4818. Branches all over. Social and counselling for widows, widowers and their children. Help with emotional, practical and financial problems. Various informative pamphlets including *Work for Widows*, *Training and Employment*, *Schools with Foundations and Grants for Widows' Children*, etc.

DHSS (*Child Benefit*), Poulton-le-Fylde, Blackpool FY6 8NW. For all queries about the special unsupported parents' Child Benefit Increase. Or get Leaflet CH 1 at Post Office, which includes a tear-off claim form.

Dr Barnardo's, Tanner's Lane, Barkingside, Ilford, Essex, 01-551 0011. Regional divisions throughout Britain. General support. Grants and loans in times of crisis. Holiday clubs, flats, caravans, children's summer camp. For referred families (Social Services).

Dr Barnardo's/Cruse, 5 Portland Terrace, Newcastle-upon-Tyne NE2 1QQ Newcastle 81524. Offers social work service in addition to statutory provision. Service extended to all single parents and their families. Write, telephone or call, 9 a.m. to 5 p.m. Mondays to Fridays.

Fairbridge Society, 119/125 N.E. Wing, Bush House, Aldwych, London WC2, 01-240 0688/9. Advice on emigration to Australia for single parents and their children. Assisted passages. Will help with schools, work, accommodation.

Families Need Fathers, 97c Shakespeare Walk, London N16 8TB. Fathers needing advice on custody, care and control – or anything else – can find it here. Monthly talk-ins held in London – to which mothers are also welcomed.

Family Care, 1 Plantagenet Street, Nottingham, Nottingham 51805. Formerly Council for Moral Welfare and still in part an adoption society, this organization extends help to any Nottingham families who make contact. It is mainly within the sphere of what they call 'social and emotional deprivation' that contact with single-parent families is made.

Family First, The Croft, Alexandra Park, Nottingham, NG3 4JD. A voluntary housing association and registered charity. Aims to provide help with accommodation for unsupported parents within the Nottingham area. Houses, flats, bed-sitters. Good-as-new shops for clothing, furniture, bedding. Play schemes for school holidays. Nursery. Emergency help service for tenants. '*Family First* respects the right of all people to a home, privacy, peace and a place in their local neighbourhood or community.'

Family Fund (Rowntree), PO Box 50, York. Helps families with handicapped children through the provision of material aids, goods, services or money grants. Referral only through Social Services.

Family Rights Group (telephone help service), 01-733 4245. Immediate advice if children are (or are about to be) taken into care. Ask for Jeremy Weinstein.

Fifth Demand Group, 214 Stapleton Hall Road, London N4. Campaigns for changes in women's taxation, National Insurance, Social Security, etc. Also individual counselling on relevant money matters.

Finer Joint Action Committee, 225 Kentish Town Road, London NW5 2LX. Presses for governmental recognition of one-parent families as a special group. Cash, day-care, housing etc., it's all their concern.

Free Representation Unit, First Floor, 3 Middle Temple Lane, Middle Temple, London EC4. Sympathetic barristers will act for you, free, in certain tribunal cases. Send outline information in first instance.

Gingerbread, 35 Wellington Street, London WC2, 01-240 0953. Groups now flourishing in almost every corner of Britain. Social, supportive, self-help, baby-sitting, toy pools, legal and other advice, holiday swap list, emergency accommodation. Various information sheets. Always available (weekdays, office hours) for consultation.

Gingerbread Advice Centre (Wales), 68 Rhosddu Road, Wrexham, Clwyd, Wrexham 57147. Help with all matters: legal, financial, emotional, environmental. Holiday register.

Gingerbread Holidays, Lloyds Bank Chambers, Camborne, Cornwall, Camborne 715901. Aims to help all types of single-parent families to get a holiday for as low a cost as possible. Hotels, holiday camps, caravans, flats, shares. Exchanges too. Inexpensive paying guest holidays offered by individuals: mainly seaside/country.

Home Office, Whitehall, London SW1A 2AP, 01-213 3000. Can authorize screening of ports and airports in a crisis.

Housing Corporation, Maple House, 149 Tottenham Court Road, London WIP OBN, 01-387 9466. Branches all over the country. Responsible for registering all housing associations which, in turn, provide us with flats, shared homes, co-ownership schemes. Understanding help always.

Job Centres are run nationally. There is one in every area. Advice on availability of local training schemes, grants, day-care, as well as employment. Telephone book for yours.

Law Society, 113 Chancery Lane, London WC2A 1PL, 01-242 1222. Use in the event of queries, complaints, confusion in respect of any legal matter, including solicitor trouble.

Legal Action Group (LAG), 28a Highgate Road, London NW5 1NS, 01-267 0048 or 01-485 1189. Produces an annual directory of legal advice and law centres. Any CAB will let you have a look at this list, or you can buy it for 50p. Or contact LAG direct for details of your nearest centre. Some run a twenty-four-hour service.

Life, 35 Kenilworth Road, Leamington Spa, Warwickshire, Leamington Spa 21587. 130 local branches throught the country. Help offered to all pregnant women regardless of marital status. Accommodation with friendly families. Hostels in seven areas. Furnishings, bedding, baby clothes and equipment. Re-housing pressure. Friendship and support. *Life Housing Trust* provides a limited number of flats, bed-sitters and hostel accommodation.

Lifeline Pregnancy Care, Highfield, Kirmond Road, Binbrook, Lincoln LN3 6DS. Befriending. Accommodation. Counselling. A service for all mothers, married or unmarried.

Liverpool Gingerbread, 4 Bold Place, Liverpool L1 9DN, 051-708 8848. Deserves a special mention. Full-time staff deal with problems and information. Arts and Crafts Centre, boat for teenagers, painting and decorating for one-parent houses/flats (Job Creation Scheme), shop; all as extras to usual social, self-help and support.

Marie Stopes, Room 7, 108 Whitfield Street, London W1, 01-388 0662 Family Planning and advice on sterilization, abortion, pregnancy testing and menopausal problems. Small charge.

Marriage Guidance Council, Little Church Street, Rugby, Warwickshire. Branches in almost every town throughout Britain. You don't have to be married to qualify for help. Mainly for emotional problems. No charge. Telephone book for local office.

Mothers' Union, Mary Sumner House, Tufton Street, London SWIP 3RB, 01-222 5533. Offers immediate succour in times of crisis. Will get children away for a holiday, or parent away for re-charging and rest, within twenty-four hours of an urgent appeal. Understanding families work across countrywide network. Open to all: married, unmarried, Christian, non-Christian, women and men. Social meetings, spiritual support, exchange-help. Enormous understanding, and nobody pressures you to conform.

NACRO, 125 Kennington Park Road, London SE11, 01-735 1151. Countrywide support group, essentially self-help and supportive, for prisoners' wives and children. Social, welfare and information. Local Probation Office for details of nearest meetings. Also produces leaflet, *Prisoners' Families*, free.

National Association of Widows, c/o Stafford District Voluntary Service Centre, Chell Road, Stafford ST1 2QA. Provides training programme for members who would like to become voluntary counsellors to other widows. All districts.

National Childminding Association, Camrie, Brasted, Westerham, Kent. Forms a liaison between regional groups and encourages new ones. Promotes training schemes for daily-minders.

National Children's Bureau, 8 Wakley Street, London EC1V 7QE. 01-278 9441/7. Responsible for two in-depth reports on one-parenting. Offers indirect help by funnelling queries to appropriate organization. Holds interesting one-day seminars on all aspects of child care. Sometimes expensive: ask for reduction on account of being an impoverished one-parent and see what happens. Open to individual membership. Use of extensive library. Coffee bar. Good place for meeting.

National Children's Home, 85 Highbury Park, London N5 1UD, 01-226 2033. Advice and counselling. Moral support. Some material provision, but rarely cash. Limited number of flats with day nursery attached.

National Council for the Divorced and Separated, 35 Parliament Hill, Hampstead, London NW3 2TA, 01-435 5831. Welfare, advisory service, social. Voluntary welfare consultants will help any divorced or separated person, whether member or not.

Penfriend scheme for isolated one-parents. Regular bulletin with members' news, council's activities: highlights current and proposed legislation affecting divorced and separated. Small subscription.

National Council for One Parent Families, 255 Kentish Town Road, London NW5 2LX, 01-267 1361. This is tops for us. The pity is that this organization is London-based only. We could do with branches, like banks, in every High Street. Margaret Bramall, its director, brought up her own family single-handed and is one of the most sympathetic and positive beings on the face of the earth. She also fights, so that the Council isn't just another 'advice centre', it is also a pressure group. Help and an ear extended to all single-parents. Easy atmosphere, prompt attention and a bag of cot blankets there in the waiting room for any parent to take. Occasional one-off grants. Has a fortnightly law centre. Holiday guide.

National Educational Research and Development Trust, 25, St Andrew's Street, Cambridge, 0223-59126. Runs hot-line help on all child problems, including battering. Welfare experts on hand to answer telephone calls. Operating in Nottingham, Manchester, Derby, Leeds and London. Known as *Parent Lifeline* (telephone book).

National Federation of Solo Clubs, Room 8, Ruskin Chambers, 191 Corporation Street, Birmingham B4 6RY, 021-236 2879. Advice centre, social welfare worker attached. Group holidays for members. Parents and children eligible for holiday grants if need great.

National Foster Care Association, 129 Queen's Crescent, London NW5 4HE, 01-485 3929. Will advise on all aspects of fostering, private and local authority. Keeps register of holiday exchanges.

National Pre-School Playgroups Association, Alford House, Aveline Road, London SE11, 01-582 8871. Welcomes inquiries from individual parents seeking help or advice.

National Society for Mentally Handicapped Children, Pembridge Hall, 17 Pembridge Square, London W2 4EP, 01-229 8941. Practical help and comfort. Conferences for interested parents. Holidays, summer camps, temporary foster care for retarded children of all ages. Quarterly magazine, *Parents' Voice*.

National Society for the Prevention of Cruelty to Children,
1 Riding House Street, London WIP 8AA, 01-580 8812. For help
in the face of physical violence to children, or to self in the
presence of children. Or any other pressing worries. Local, un-
uniformed officers will usually give instant succour. See your
telephone book.

National Women's Aid Federation, 51 Chalcot Road, London NW1,
01-586 0104/5194. Provides (countrywide, not, as generally
supposed, London only) refuges for battered women and their
children. Or will simply talk, sympathize and advise over the
telephone.

Network, 23 Hand Court (off High Holborn), London WC1,
01-504 3001. For advice on legal problems relating to
handicapped children.

New Opportunities Course, Department of Adult Education,
University of Newcastle-upon-Tyne. Pioneers of full-day courses
tailored to fit in with school hours, aimed at 'personal
reorientation'. For women (and men) who have been out of
action for some years while raising a family. Politics, literature,
psychology, philosophy, English and 'Women in Society'. Also
held at Nottingham, Manchester and Hatfield so far.

North Tyneside Single Parents' Family Groups, c/o Council
for Voluntary Service, 96 High Street, Wallsend, Northumberland,
Wallsend 261794. Social and self-help groups: welfare advice.

One Parent Family Holidays (Continental), 25 Fore Street,
Praze-an-Beeble, Cambourne, Cornwall. For best-value-for-money
holidays abroad: parents and children. Half-term and school
holidays. Also parents-alone breaks to the continent.

Open University (Admissions Office), PO Box 48, Milton Keynes,
MK7 6AB. For degree or single courses. No previous academic
qualifications needed. Apply up till June for degree courses;
between April and October for associates. One of the most
satisfactory methods of home-study.

Paddington Neighbourhood Law Centre, 465 Harrow Road,
London W10, 01-960 4481. Will provide you with a do-it-yourself
Injunction Kit for 25p.

Parents Anonymous is a telephone help service for mother and
father who need urgent advice. Violence towards children perhaps?
Evenings from 6 p.m. and weekends. Middlesex area,
(092 74) 23483.

Parents for Children, 222 Camden High Street, London NW1, 01-485 7526. Will consider single people as prospective adopters.

Parents' National Education Union, Murray House, Vandon Street, London SW1, 01-222 7181. Will give help and encouragement to parents who wish to educate their children at home.

Parents Without Partners, 61 Carlisle Street, Brighton, Sussex. Social, welfare, supportive.

Passport Office, Clive House, 70–78 Petty France, London SW1H 9HD, 01-222 8010. Will answer any queries related to the issue of passports and travel documents on behalf of children.

Richmond Churches Housing Trust, 9 Sheen Gate, London SW14 7PD. Especially sympathetic towards one-parent families. Interdenominational. A caring group who visit and 'take an interest' as well as keeping roofs over heads.

Rights of Women, 2 St Paul's Road, London N1, 01-359 6656. Campaigning organization eager to help on all financial, 'claims' and legal questions. Publishes useful booklets. Invaluable to all who live on SB.

Sailors' Children's Society, Newland, Hull HU6 7RJ, Hull 423312/3. Supports one-parent families at home. Financial aid, either ongoing, lump sum or incidental, according to need. Advice on housing, schools, relationships and children's behaviour problems. Jerseys provided at Christmas. Open to children of seafarers only. Application direct or through Social Services or relevant organizations.

Salvation Army, 101 Queen Victoria Street, London EC4P 4EP, 01-236 7020. That address for 'Goodwill Department'. But Women's Social Services from 280 Mare Street, Hackney, London E8 1HE, 01-985 1181/4 and 01-985 1801. Practical aid to any needy person. Playgroups, children's clubs, surgeries, advice bureaux, meals for children, day nurseries, clothing centres, accommodation for homeless families, visits to prisoners' families, holidays for tired mothers and for 'underprivileged children and their families', hostels for working women with pre-school children and more. The Family Service and Inquiry Department concentrates on helping parents find missing partners. They will assist with reconciliation where practicable or advise on affiliation and maintenance matters. Branches throughout the country. Telephone book.

Samaritans answer telephone calls from the despairing (not necessarily suicidal) any time of day or night. Local telephone book or headquarters at St Stephen's Church (crypt), Walbrook, London EC4, 01-626 9000.

Save the Children Fund, Jebb House, 157 Clapham Road, London SW9 OPT, 01-582 1414. Advisory service. Clubs play-bus (London). Play centres and groups. Mainly in London, but plenty in provincial cities too. Practical help for child-minders.

Second Start. These courses are run as adult education programmes, usually at technical colleges during school hours. How to meet problems related to taxation, DHSS allowances, specialist organizations and services, personal and emotional struggles, child care and legal matters. Instigated by a single parent. Crèche usually available. Information from Liz Parsons at Somerset College of Arts and Technology, Wellington Road, Taunton TA1 5AX (sae please). Courses at present running at Taunton, Wellington, Bristol, Trowbridge and Brecon. Others will follow (urge your own tech for local courses).

SHAC (London Housing Aid Centre), 189a Old Brompton Road, London SW5, 01-373 7276. A service for all London families with (or expecting) children. Help on homelessness, eviction, 'bad housing', moving out to New Towns. An emergency team helps with finding temporary accommodation in times of crisis. Telephone for guidance, or if problems are complicated make an appointment for consultation. Children welcomed to office.

Shelter, 157 Waterloo Road, London SE1 8UU, 01-633 9377. All help and advice on housing matters.

Singlehanded Ltd, 68 Lewes Road, Haywards Heath, Sussex, Haywards Heath 54663. Helps lone fathers and mothers to find homes to share with contemporaries. Finds and places housekeepers and substitute mothers. Organizes group holidays and 'children only' holidays. Penfriends and companionship too.

Singles Holidays Ltd, 23 Abingdon Road, London W8, 01-937 0102. For single people, including single parents, who want to have a holiday away from the children.

Social Responsibility Council (Quakers), Friends' House, Euston Road, London NW1 2BJ, 01-387 3601. Housing associations at Hull, Tunbridge Wells, Birmingham, Colchester, Loughborough and Stroud. Short-term homes, flatlets-plus-warden, and nine units served by an integral nursery so that mothers may go out to work.

Sunderland Council for Voluntary Service (SPIN), 56 Frederick Street, Sunderland, Sunderland 78902. Single-parent groups throughout the district. Social, welfare and self-help.

Supplementary Benefits Commission, New Court, Carey Street, London WC2A 2LS, 01-831 6111. This is the seat of the DHSS. Let them have your problems, general and particular.

Thomas Coram Foundation, 40 Brunswick Square, London WCIN IAZ, 01-278 2424. Advice on fostering and adoption: all areas. Day care, mothers' circle, child health clinic, social worker service, library, toy lending, launderette. Only for families living in adjacent area.

Toc H, 1 Forest Close, Wendover, Aylesbury, Bucks. Will arrange holidays for physically handicapped children. Accommodation for parents too, very often, if they're willing to help.

TOPS (Training Services Agency), Telford House, Hamilton Close, Basingstoke, Hants RG21 2UZ. For information on whereabouts of courses, grants available and choice of subjects.

Toy Libraries Association, Toynbee Hall, 28 Commercial Street, London EI. Helps to initiate local groups throughout the country. Maintains links with therapists, teachers, research workers, art colleges and manufacturers. Publishers newsletter and toy index. Available for normal and handicapped children.

Vineyard Project, Congregational Church Crypt, The Vineyard, Richmond, Surrey, 01-940 2965. Day/evening centre for adults and children. Social, sport, hobbies, classes. Problems sorted out. Limited housing available for single-parent families. Also single-parents' *Survival Course*.

Women's Royal Voluntary Service, 17 Old Park Lane, London WIY 4AJ, 01-499 6040. Negotiates country holidays for needy children. Can provide help for remaining parent if mother/father in long-stay in hospital. Can give tired or sick mother a rest away from children. Visits lonely or problem-ridden parents for friendship/support. Good second-hand furniture, bedding, equipment, clothing. On recommendation of Social Services, Gingerbread, etc.

Youth Hostels Association, Trevelyan House, 8 St Stephen's Hill, St Albans, Herts ALI 2DY, St Albans 55215. One of the cheapest and healthiest means of taking a holiday with the children. No children under five. Unaccompanied children from twelve years upwards. No upper age limit, in spite of the 'Youth' bit.

Index